NEXT LEVEL LIVING

PRINCIPLES THAT ELEVATE AND ENHANCE YOUR LIFE

DR. TAMIKA FORD

NEXT LEVEL LIVING

ISBN:978-0-578-45311-8

Next Level International
P.O. Box 38451
Shreveport, La 71133
www.tamikaford.com

TABLE OF CONTENTS

INTRODUCTION

One of my strongest convictions in life is that every human being has a responsibility to discover their true identity and fulfill their God-given purpose while here on earth. For this to happen, you must possess a passion for growth. Growth allows you to evolve into the person God has created you to be. There is no progress without growth. If we're not growing, we're dying; if we're not progressing, we're regressing. There's no in between. Most people will eventually drift backward if they don't decide to move forward.

Deciding to change your life is the first step toward personal development. Each one of us has an opportunity to be extraordinary if we are willing to put in the time, effort, and energy that is required. Will you choose to be great? Are you ready to take the necessary steps to shift your life to greater heights? It's time to advance to the next level and experience the abundant life.

When you're pursuing next level living, it will challenge you to face your fears, and force you out of your comfort zone. I need you to get comfortable with being uncomfortable. This is the only way to see substantial growth in your life. You must be committed to the growth process to experience the results you desire. A commitment will allow you to overcome the obstacles and barriers that have been hindering your progress for way too long. Without dedication and commitment, there will be no advancement.

I decided to pursue growth seven years ago, and it's the best decision I've ever made besides surrendering my life to Christ. It's been life-changing for me. During my journey, I have discovered my identity and purpose in life. I'm a new person with new ideas and new ways of doing things.

My relationship with God is stronger than ever before, and I acknowledge Him in all that I do. We must be willing to surrender our old ways of doing things and embrace the newness that God has prepared for all of us. God's desire is for us to grow in our faith so that we can move to the next phase of our lives.

How can we serve others if we fail to develop ourselves? It's impossible. When you grow, then you can help other people grow. But you can't share what you don't know. Obtain the knowledge you need to improve your life and the lives of others. No knowledge, no growth. We can never develop beyond our level of understanding. To flourish in life, we need wisdom. And true wisdom only comes from God. His knowledge is pure, loving, peaceful, and gentle. It gives you the desire to do good works and live an honorable life. **Proverbs 4:7** declares, "Wisdom is the principal thing; therefore, get wisdom: and with all thy getting get understanding." Without wisdom, we are walking blindly through life relying on others to give us meaning and purpose in life.

After reading this book, I hope that you will be motivated and inspired to shift your life to new dimensions. There are certain attributes that you must possess for this to occur. In this book, I share some fundamental principles that you need to cultivate to experience real growth in your life. Some of the qualities summarized in this book are character, love, honor, humility, and forgiveness. When you embody these characteristics, you will experience the abundant life—a life of peace, joy, fulfillment, contentment, and satisfaction. Study these traits and practice them daily. When you apply these principles, expect to see increase. You're guaranteed to yield amazing fruit in your life. Are you ready to live on the next level?

Next Level Living

4

CHAPTER 1

DISCOVERING IDENTITY: WHO AM I?

Who are you? Do you know who you are? If we fail to seek the answer to this question, we'll find ourselves subscribing to other people's opinions, ideas, and philosophies of who we should be. We shouldn't look to others for definition and constant validation. They don't have the answers to who we are, and – frankly—the majority of people don't have a clue as to who they are. Every human question their identity at some point of their existence; however, his or her true self will only be discovered through exploration. One has to choose to take a journey of self-discovery. That journey begins with God. He has the key to your identity. Man did not create you; therefore, man doesn't have the answer to the question "Who am I?"

DISCOVER

For a real understanding of who we are, we must look to our creator. Look into the truth of God's word and use it as a mirror to understand your identity. God labels us. **2 Corinthians 1:22** reads, "...*And He has identified us as His own by placing the Holy Spirit in our hearts as the first installment that guarantees* *everything he has promised us.*" It's dangerous to look to others for identity, instead of God. We'll find deceit. We shouldn't rely on other people to define us because they didn't create us. And what if they get it wrong? What if they identify you as someone that God never created you to be? So now you're strolling around impersonating someone else, trying to be something or someone that God never intended you to be. All because you listened to the wrong voices.

When you're unaware of who you are, you become susceptible to another person's definition of who they think you are or what they think you're supposed to be. When this happens, your identity is determined by the various relationships you have in the current season. So, how you perceive yourself now changes with each new relationship. What a tragedy, but it happens when we're clueless of our own identity. It's not the next person's responsibility or burden to always affirm you or define who you are. This is not how God intended us to discover our true identity.

True identity is discovered through our pursuit of God. We have to seek, chase, and pursue our maker to know and understand who we are because He is our Creator. Only the Creator knows the true essence of His creation and a designer knows the intent of their design. We were created and designed by God, made in his image; therefore, it is difficult to know yourself outside of God. **Genesis 1:27** announces, "*So God created man in his own image; in the*

image of God created he him; male and female created he them."
Your identity is wrapped up in the Creator, and so the process of
finding yourself starts with Him.

It is God who knew us before we entered the earth. God
knew us before we were formed in our mother's womb (**Jer. 1:5**).
Our identity was determined before we entered the world. This is
good to know. Now we understand that it is God who has the key
to our identity. No more relying on people to define you. God
validates you.

VALIDATION

Are you always needing other people to validate you,
affirm you, or approve you? I need you to seriously think about
this because we shouldn't need another person's approval to feel
good and confident about who God made us to be. Our true essence
stems from the inside and not the outside. We're not defined by
our friendships, careers, titles, possessions, material wealth, or the
opinions of others. We are defined by God alone; therefore, we
shouldn't spend any time, energy, effort or resources trying to
justify ourselves to others. Your need to be affirmed continuously
by others is an indication of low self-worth. If you're struggling
with low self-esteem, all the validation in the world will not fill
that void of you not knowing God or your true self-worth. God
validates you and provides meaning and purpose to your life, not
people.

Total fulfillment is only found in God and nowhere else. Our wholeness, satisfaction, joy, and peace are all derived from our relationship with Him. I always like to say that we have this God-sized hole in our souls that can only be filled by God. If we fail to allow Him to fill that void in our hearts, we'll continue to wander through life feeling empty. People may provide you with temporary satisfaction and fulfillment, but it's incredibly short-lived. We were not designed to complete one another. That is God's job, and no other human being can fill that position. When we look to others to do things they were never designed or powerless to do, we set ourselves up for disappointment. These are misplaced expectations that need to be adjusted. It's not fair to the other person(s) to be expected to do things they are incapable of executing. Once we allow God to make us whole, our understanding of who we are is more evident, and now we can modify our expectations. We begin to view ourselves and other people differently.

YOUR VIEW

How do you view yourself? Do you see yourself the way God sees you or do you view yourself in light of your past mistakes and failures? This is a very significant question that must be answered because your progress and next level is predicated on how you feel about yourself. Maintaining a positive self-image is very important; for it affects your self-esteem and confidence. It doesn't matter how other people view you. What matters the most is how you perceive yourself. People may say that you're great, gifted, talented, and awesome; however, if you don't see it, or if you don't believe it, then it's not true for you. You have to believe that you were created in the image of God and that you're a unique individual destined for greatness. It all starts with self-perception.

Never associate your past mistakes with who you are. The failures and shortcomings of your past does not define who you are. We've all engaged in activities that we're not proud of; however, those things don't determine our identity. There's always an opportunity to grow and change. For example, previously, I was an alcoholic. I'm not proud of that title; nonetheless, that was my behavior in the past. Drinking too much alcohol is what I *used to do*. I can't change the past; however, the past doesn't define me. I've taken advantage of the opportunity to change my life, and now I have some control over what happens in my future. You can do the same.

When you associate your past behavior with who you are, you will begin to reject who God has made you to be. Did you know that who you are and how you were designed is directly connected to your purpose? So, when you reject you, you reject purpose. I need you to realize that you were uniquely designed and handcrafted by God. You're an original, and that's what makes you unique. There's no one else on earth that has the same set of fingerprints as you. There's no one else that can be you like you or do life the way that you do it. We're all different but great in our own way.

In the Bible, the writer Paul affirms that we are God's masterpiece (**Ephesians 2:10**). The word "masterpiece" is defined as an artist's greatest piece of work or outstanding work of art. We are God's greatest piece of artwork. Wow, what a compliment! If we fail to deal with the negative issues that are hindering our development, we'll never uncover our true self— God's masterpiece. Before we can truly grow and become who God has created us to be, we must rid ourselves of the negative baggage. Hidden deep down under all of that baggage is a diamond eagerly waiting to be discovered.

SORT IT OUT

We have an identity crisis, and it's time to sort out the issues that are affecting many areas of our lives. There are negative experiences from our past that still affect us today. When we refuse to face these issues, they can affect our relationship with our friends, parents, children, school, work, and church. Whatever you are grappling with from your past must be addressed immediately. The sooner we attend to these problems, the faster our lives will begin to turn for the better. Yes, it's a process, but we must get started.

What are you wrestling with today? Some of us may be dealing with parent issues, sibling issues, neglect, abandonment, rejection, abuse, or insecurities from our childhood. Whatever your problem may be, remember that God is willing and ready to help you. It's time to sort out the baggage that's been weighing you down and impeding your progress. You've been carrying around this luggage of issues for way too long, and God is ready to start the healing process so that you can finally be set free. In **Matthew 11:28-30** Jesus declares,

> *"Come unto me, all ye that labour and are heavy laden, and I will give you rest. Take my yoke upon you and learn of me; for I am meek and lowly in heart: and ye shall find rest unto your souls. For my yoke is easy, and my burden is light."*

In this text, we see Jesus is ready to help us unload. He wants to put our souls to rest, but we must be willing to hand over our burdens. Surrender!

Are you ready to surrender your baggage of the past over to God? It might be the baggage of pain, the baggage of not forgiving, the baggage of rejection, or the baggage of bitterness. Whatever you're battling, surrender it over to God and allow Him to heal you. For this to happen, you must be honest and truthful with yourself. Admit that you have a problem and be willing to face your issues. It's time to be real with yourself. You'll never change what you don't confront. Be willing to face the matters that are preventing you from discovering your true essence. Confront the issues that are delaying your development and hindering forward progress. When we choose not to heal or forgive people and situations, we are choosing to remain in pain. We are choosing to suffer and harbor bitterness. Don't do this to yourself. It's time to be free. Allow God to cleanse you.

SPRING CLEANING

We are in need of a spiritual spring-cleaning. Our hearts are congested with all the wrong junk. It's time for us to detoxify our souls of all the darkness, hate, hurt, disappointment, and bitterness that's been clogging our hearts for way too long. God wants to purify, cleanse, and restore our hearts to newness. This all begins by renewing our minds to God's way of doing things. We have to feed our minds new spiritual food. The old food has been hurting us and leading us down the wrong path. Time to change your diet.

If we desire to transform our lives, our old way of thinking must be discarded. We must reprogram our thinking and make sure it lines up with the truth. When you shift your thinking and allow your thoughts to line up with the mind of God, transformation takes place. God instructs us not to be *"conformed to this world:*

but be ye transformed by the renewing of your mind, that ye may prove what is that good, and acceptable, and perfect, will of God" **(Romans 12:2).** Change your thinking, and you can change your life. It's that simple, but not always easy to do. It will require work, and you must be committed to the growth process.

I don't want to minimize what has happened to you in the past, but you must change how you think about the things that have affected you. The way you think about the people and situations from the past determines your freedom today. For instance, my mother gave birth to me when she was only fourteen years old; therefore, my grandmother took the responsibility of rearing me. As I grew older, I began to resent my mother. I later developed feelings of abandonment because my grandmother raised me and my mother did not. I felt like it was my mother's responsibility to take care of me. I translated her not being there for me as her not loving me. So, for years I thought my mother rejected me and that she didn't love me. I remember saying to myself, "If my mother really loved me, why didn't she take the responsibility of nurturing me?" At the time, I didn't understand that my grandmother was better equipped to care for me. I was blessed, and I didn't even know it.

Later in life, when I matured and gained some perspective, I was now grateful that my grandmother reared me. My old way of thinking had been discarded, and I became free from the negative thoughts and perceptions of my past. Now, I had an understanding of why my mother chose not to rear me. She did not have the knowledge or the capability of nurturing a young life, especially when she was yet a child herself. My perspective changed, and I began to feel empathy for my mother because I realized that she did the best she knew how at that time. When I altered my thinking, it caused me to have a different outlook. I no longer harbored those negative emotions about my mother because I decided to shift my thinking. Once again, you must be willing to change how you think in order to transform your life. It all starts with your thoughts!

YOUR MINDSET

For you to become the person that God has created you to be, you must adjust your mindset. Your way of thinking must reflect the mind of God. Michael Michalko, an internationally acclaimed creative thinking expert, asserted, "If you always think the way you've always thought, you will always get what you've always got – the same old same old." What a true statement. Right thinking leads to right actions.

What have you been thinking about lately? Everything you do, your actions, attitude, and responses are all initiated by a thought. If you think on it long enough, actions will undoubtedly follow. The Bible asserts, *"As a man thinks in his heart, so is he"*

(Proverbs 23:7). In other words, whatever you continue to meditate on is what you become. If you continuously ponder on the hurt and pain others caused you, you run the risk of becoming the very thing you hate in others. They caused you pain, so now you're causing someone else pain because you never forgave or dealt with the hurt. You continued to replay the offenses in your mind, which led to unwise choices and decisions. This could be avoided if we just refuse to permit the wrong thoughts to settle in our souls.

Be careful not to allow the pain of your past to consume your mind. Pinpoint the issues that produced the suffering in your life and seek God's way of dealing with those matters. God desires for us to be healthy, both spiritually and mentally. All of our battles in life begin in our minds. Our thoughts influence our actions, which in turn create our experiences. If you can win the battle in your mind, you can win the battle in life. When negative thoughts that are contrary to truth appear in your mind, discard them, and replace those thoughts with words of truth. **2 Corinthians 10:4-5** warns,

> *"For the weapons of our warfare are not carnal, but mighty through God to the pulling down of strong holds;) Casting down imaginations, and every high thing that exalteth itself against the knowledge of God and bringing into captivity every thought to the obedience of Christ."*

This can be an ongoing battle at times, but you must fight and not give up. Your transformation depends on it. Once your life starts to reflect your renewed mind, your relationships will begin to improve. How you relate, respond, and interact with others will gradually change. You will no longer find it necessary to compare yourself to others, which is definitely unwise. Why is there a need to compare yourself to others when there is only one of you? No one can do you or be you better than you.

When you change your mindset and focus on discovering your true identity, you lose the desire to compete with other people. We're not here to compete with each other. We should be helping each other, building each other up, and sharing each other's burdens. Compete with yourself and become better this year than you were last year. Strive to be better today than you were yesterday. Become the best version of yourself and develop every area of your life. Become the person that God has called you to be, and not who others think you should be.

Learn how to commend others and celebrate their accomplishments. Refusing to compliment or rejoice with other individuals is a mark of low self-esteem. It indicates that you may have a negative self- image or simply don't know who you are. Either way, it's an identity crisis, and we need to obtain the necessary information to make critical changes in our lives. It's difficult to make changes without the proper knowledge to do so.

GET KNOWLEDGE

For you to become who God has intended you to be, knowledge has to be obtained. Knowledge is just information. We need the right information to bring about a change in our lives. Change can only happen when we change the information that we have. We can never rise above our level of knowledge. In order to go higher, we must gain new information. Knowledge is necessary. You can't do what you don't know.

Pursue God for the wisdom you need to transform your life. Nothing changes for the better in your life, until you are enlightened about who you really are. This is why the Bible declares, "*Wisdom is the principal thing; therefore get wisdom: and with all thy getting get understanding*" (**Proverbs 4:7**). Gain an understanding of who God made you to be so that you can carry out His plan and purpose for your life. I like a quote by Donald Rumsfeld, which says, "*You don't know [what] you don't know.*" This is the reason we have to seek out the information we need to discover what we do not know.

When you know better, you have an opportunity to do better. How can we enhance our lives if we lack the information to do so? We must get informed. If you fail to seek out the knowledge you need to develop yourself and discover your identity, you place yourself in a dangerous predicament. When this happens, you have to rely on others to speculate who they think you are and what they think you should be doing with your life. How frightening is this? These people did not create you; therefore, they don't have the insight into who you are and what you were designed to become.

I often hear people say, "What you don't know will not hurt you." I disagree. I believe what we don't know can damage us immensely. For example, if I lack the knowledge I need to manage my finances, I run the risk of experiencing great financial debt, stress, anxiety and the loss of relationships from not paying my debts. This can be damaging to my life; however, if I obtain the right information to manage my finances, it will alleviate most of the issues noted above. Refusing to attain the information you need to change critical situations in your life has the potential to ruin you.

When you don't know the truth, how can you apply it to your life? Many people are defeated and destroyed because they lack knowledge (**Hosea 4:6**). Notice Hosea didn't say a lack of career, lack of wealth, or lack of friends. No. He said a lack of knowledge has the potential to destroy your life. It will definitely hinder your development and your next level. We all need the truth about who we really are and what God has called us to do in this world. Only the truth will set us free. Knowledge allows us to be our true authentic selves and be free from the need to be constantly validated and affirmed by others. When you know who you are, then you understand who you are not. Only the truth can give you such a revelation. *"And ye shall know the truth, and the truth shall make you free"* (**John 8:32**).

Questions for Discussion & Reflection:

1. After reading this Chapter, what insight did you receive as it relates to your Identity?

2. Who Are You? Do you know who God has called you to be?

3. Is your Identity wrapped up in your career, education, titles, performance, etc.?

4. Are you ready to take a journey of self-discovery? How can you begin to find your true identity as it relates to who God has called you to be?

5. What baggage from your past is hindering you from discovering your true identity?

6. Who are you seeking to establish your identity or validate you? Is it your spouse, friends, relatives, colleagues, church people, etc.?

7. Search deep within and ask yourself if you're happy and content with the person you have become presently. Does that person reflect the image and likeness of God?

CHAPTER 2

DEVELOPING YOUR CHARACTER

According to Merriam-Webster, character is "the group of qualities that make a person, group, or thing different from others." Character is the way a person reasons, feels, and acts. The choices and decisions that are made when no one is watching typically exemplify the real you. Most of us tend to make better decisions when others are watching to protect our reputations. For some reason, we want people to think of us in a particular manner; therefore, we behave the way others think we should. I personally know people that act a certain way when others are watching, but behind closed doors, they are a completely different person. This is hypocritical behavior.

A hypocrite is a person that says one thing and does another. Often, their words are not consistent with their actions or deeds. A person of integrity will be consistent regardless of where they are and who they are with. They will not change. One of the ways to test a person's character is by observing how they treat the people whom they have authority or advantage over.

Malcolm Forbes, the publisher of Forbes magazine, states, *"You can easily judge the character of a man by how he treats those who can do nothing for him."* Character is one of the most important things we possess. A person's nature and temperament will sustain them and determine the course of their lives. The condition of our hearts can be perceived by our actions, attitudes, reactions, and responses; therefore, it's imperative that we consider our thoughts before we speak and take action.

Our words and actions are manifestations of our thought life. Be mindful of the seeds you allow to be planted in your heart and mind. The wrong seeds will contaminate the heart and eventually be reflected in your way of life. Your goal is to maintain a pure heart. Even when we do good things, we need to make sure they are done with the right motives in mind. Sometimes we think no one knows our heart, but we must remember that God sees all things. People tend to look at our outward appearance, but God looks at our hearts (**1 Sam 16:7**).

Since most of us say and act out the issues that reside in our hearts, we must make a conscious effort to guard and protect our hearts. The scripture warns us to *"Keep thy heart with all diligence; for out of it are the issues of life"* (**Proverbs 4:23**). We safeguard our hearts by being mindful of the ideas we allow to be planted into our minds. The seeds that are planted in your heart will eventually become your words and then your actions. If good seeds are planted in your spirit, good actions will usually follow.

The type of seeds you allow to be planted into your heart is very critical to your future; therefore, you must protect your spirit from corruptible seeds. For instance, if you have friends that always want to berate or criticize other people, then you need to change the topic of discussion when they start to condemn others in your presence. If not, their bad habits of attacking others will eventually rub off on you. Their behavior will influence you. This could result in you being labeled a slanderer or gossip. People will not trust you, and this can cause you to lose very significant relationships. The Bible tells us that "bad company corrupts good character." So, to guard your heart, you must be mindful of the places you go, the people you entertain, the conversations you engage in, and the events you attend.

Whether we believe this or not, the people that we spend the most time with have a significant influence over on lives. These associations usually determine how far we travel in life. Be attentive to the individuals you choose to spend the majority of your time with. This is vitally important. If we're not careful, we'll begin to think, act, respond, and speak in a manner that's similar to the people we surround ourselves with. Their positive or negative behaviors will inevitably rub off on us, knowingly or unknowingly.

Ask yourself this question, who am I lending my ears to? And what people am I allowing to speak into my life? Do these people exemplify integrity and uprightness? Do they make wise choices and decisions? These are very significant questions as it relates to the development of your character. You must remember that seeds are being planted in your heart by these individuals who you allow to influence your life. It is true that the words we consistently speak and receive from others will begin to take root in our hearts and later produce a favorable or unfavorable harvest. This affects the trajectory of our lives.

Commonly identified as a personal development legend, Jim Rohn says, "You are the average of the five people you spend the most time with." I totally agree with this statement based on my previous experiences. One day, while visiting the library, I met this lady, and I later established a close friendship with her. We had much in common, and both of us enjoyed chatting about spiritual matters. We would converse on the phone quite frequently and also participate in other activities together. I really enjoyed her company. Whenever we chatted about different topics, she would always repeat this certain phrase quite often, "Do you understand what I'm saying?" So, one day, while conversing with her, I noticed that I spoke the same phrase that she often quoted. This was mind-boggling to me. Laughing to myself, I remember thinking, "What am I saying? Those are not even my words." Her language was influencing my language because we were spending a great deal of time together. Yes, it's called influence. And no one is exempt. Now, what if this was negative dialect that I was picking up? Fortunately for me, her words and attitude were positive influences in my life.

Who are you allowing to speak into your life? We must remain conscious of our surroundings and the people we allow to impart into our lives. When we continue to permit the wrong group of individuals to sow the wrong seeds into our hearts, we will reap an unfavorable harvest that will manifest in our attitudes and actions. The scripture says "out of the heart flows the issues of your life." The heart creates issues that you will later have to deal with. Remember, your words and the words you listen to are planted in your heart, and those seeds will produce a good harvest or a bad harvest one day, so be careful.

Our character can be developed by first controlling our thoughts. There is a Chinese proverb that states, "Watch your thoughts, they become words; watch your words, they become actions; watch your actions, they become habits; watch your habits, they become character; watch your character, for it becomes your destiny." It all starts with our thinking. Whatever thoughts you continue to meditate on, actions will follow. As a man thinks in his heart, so is he (**Proverbs 23:7**). You eventually become whatever you continuously meditate on. We must continuously monitor our thinking and be aware that good thoughts lead to good actions and evil thoughts lead to evil acts. If we desire to grow and advance to the next level, we must continue to develop as individuals. Your character is who you are and not what you do. There is a difference.

GODLY CHARACTER

Having integrity has always been important to me once I formed a relationship with God. I believe, as followers of Christ, our character should reflect the nature of God. We should strive to have pure thoughts that are consistent with the word of God. It is imperative that we cultivate our thinking to reflect the mind of Christ daily, and this can only happen by renewing our minds with truth.

For our nature to reflect the nature of God, we have to develop a different mindset. The old mentality must go. We must adopt God's way of reasoning, which is a higher level of thinking. Whatever you feed your mind will always be revealed through your actions. I can observe your actions and predict your level of thinking because your way of thinking is always exposed through your behavior. Renew your mind by feeding it the principles of God. When you nourish your mind with the truth, you will begin to exhibit Godly character. The Bible teaches us that we're only transformed by the renewing of our minds (**Rom. 12:2**).

In order for us to develop a Godly nature, we must surrender our selfish desires and become committed to Christ. Following God and seeking His way of existing will always require sacrifice, but it's worth it.

The life you gain from pursuing Him will far exceed anything you ever had to give up. So, make a decision to follow Christ. And remember, there's power in your decision. Every decision you make will either empower you to progress or regress in life. The choice is yours.

Your everyday choices play a significant role in your character development. Life is choice driven. The decisions you make today will determine who you will become tomorrow. Make sure your choices, responses, and reactions line up with the principles of God. No more doing what you think is right in your own eyes. Your decisions decide your destiny! Make the right choices.

Study the nature of God and build a close and intimate relationship with Him. You cannot create a relationship with someone you do not know. It's imperative that we get acquainted with God so we can discern who He requires us to be. As children of God, our attitude and actions should resemble the Father. The Bible tells us to be imitators of God, as dear children (**Eph. 5:1**). Again, we should look like our Father. Continue to seek Godly wisdom and be consistent in your prayer life so that you can develop Christ-like character.

Christ is our model. And when we decide to follow Him, our nature begins to resemble His nature. Following Christ requires submission. We must submit to God's way of doing things if we desire to see growth and progress in our lives. When we refuse to submit, we refuse to grow. And this refusal is an indication of a prideful heart that desperately needs to be humbled. A prideful heart opposes God. When you're prideful, you're essentially saying, "I know it all and I have arrived." There is no need for improvement. This is deception because we know there's always room to learn, grow, and advance at every stage of life. Don't be deceived.

Planting the seed of God's word in your heart will always harvest good fruit. We can tell what's in a person's heart by the fruit they bear. A person with Christ-like character will always exhibit the Fruit of the Spirit, which is love, peace, joy, patience, kindness, goodness, faithfulness, meekness, and self-control. Remember, your character is the fruit of what's in your heart. We can always identify people by their fruit, that is, by the way they act (**Matthew 7:16).**

I always like to say that our fruit will identify what type of tree we are. It's not enough to just say we have good morals and values. It must also be displayed in our everyday actions for others to witness. I've discovered that our words don't mean much without the character to back them up. Basically, your words hold more weight when actions follow.

When we display Godlike characteristics, it sets an example for others to follow. This is why we have to be mindful of the decisions we make on a daily basis. Pay attention to the words you speak and the actions you display. Discipline your thoughts and your speech. Conduct yourself in a manner that reflects the nature of God. And remember, your choices will eventually become your habits. And your habits will determine what type of person you become. Good habits develop good character. What kind of habits are you developing?

Often, when we think of habits, we tend to think of the negative ones. This shouldn't always be the case. We can develop good habits such as loving others, being patient, kind, giving, compassionate, and forgiving. These good habits will cause us to develop Christ-like characteristics. Please realize that your habits help shape your character. Great habits develop great character.

If you're not forming habits that will have a positive effect on your life, then its time to make some adjustments. It's time to confront any destructive practices that are hindering your forward progress. Your habits should always align with your values and your standards in life.

ADVERSITY

As we move toward strengthening our character, we must realize that we'll all experience adversity at some point in our lives. Adversity usually shows up in the form of trials and tribulations; however, the Bible urges us to count it all joy when we're faced with various tests because our trials will produce patience and endurance in us **(James 1:2-3).** Adversity is necessary for you to grow as an individual. When everything is going well in your life, character lacks the opportunity it needs to develop and mature.

We usually fail to grow during good times because good times never require us to move out of our comfort zones. It's only when you are challenged, do you really see what's in your heart. Sometimes your reactions will surprise you. Remember, we all have blind spots. There are areas in your life that need improving that you can't see yet. Others can see it, but not you.

To be honest, we see ourselves for who we desire to be, but God sees us for who we really are. And He will reveal our blind spots to us if we are willing to see them and adjust. I now understand that experiencing hardships can be beneficial because we're able to realize our shortcomings, which gives us an opportunity to strengthen our weak areas. There's always wisdom to be gained from adversity and hardships.

The condition of your heart is always exposed when you're confronted with challenges and difficulties. Everything inside of you (good and bad) will surface to the forefront when a trial test you. Trials have the ability to refine us if we're submitted to the process of development. God wants to improve our character and shape us through these various tests and trials, but we must be willing to make the necessary changes that will enhance our lives.

Tribulations can help you identify the impurities and weaknesses that are preventing you from moving to the next level. The fire will try everyone at some point in their life. No one is exempt. The purpose of the fire is to melt away the impurities that reside in us. We all have dirt that needs to be purged out of us. This is all a part of the development process.

God desires to clean us, purify us, and purge us of all unrighteousness, which can be done when we're tried and tested. The Bible informs us of the many afflictions we will suffer in this lifetime, but it is how we respond that determines whether we grow from these experiences. If we plan to become the person that God has called us to be and do all that He has prepared for us to do, then we must be willing to develop Godly character. There's no way around it. Your life may be under construction right now, and that's okay. God is doing a work in you. Now is the time to surrender and allow Him to mold you into that great woman or man that He has created you to become.

THE RIGHT CHARACTER

Righteousness is the basis for true lasting success. I believe you are considered successful when you live according to Godly standards and follow God's purpose for your life. Some people have an abundance of money, possessions, position, power, and titles; but they lack quality character. Are they truly successful? What do they really have? Some have gained material wealth at the expense of their souls. What do you really profit if you gain the whole world, which includes money, fame, and possessions, but lose your own soul? (**Mark 8:36**). We need to embody a Godly character.

Gifts and talents will open doors for you, but your character will sustain you. It is your character that will allow you to elevate to higher levels. Your temperament can make you or break you. It's your choice. How you respond and react to circumstances and situations in life is vital. Your responses reflect your true nature. They only reveal the condition of your heart. Individuals that embody righteousness and integrity will usually respond accordingly, despite how difficult the situation may be.

Great character begins with your inner-man. Real growth and change will always start from the inside out. You can attempt to change your behavior, but if you don't change your heart or the way you think about life, then you'll eventually revert to your old ways. Behavior modification without a renewed mind is only temporary. Remember, building character requires you to work on yourself. Be willing to put in the effort and do what is necessary to develop internally. No work, no progress. This is a life-long process. Continue to grow and strive for excellence in all of your endeavors. We should be able to look at our lives and see continual progress.

GROWTH

A concept that I believe to be true is that if we are not growing, we're dying; if we're not progressing, we're regressing; and if we're not getting better, we're getting worse. There is no in-between. Most people will eventually drift backward if they don't decide to move forward in their lives. We must stay committed to the process of spiritual and personal development. I always like to say, "If you know better, then you have an opportunity to do better." I say this because knowing better doesn't always mean we will actually do better, but knowledge does give us the opportunity to improve our lives.

It's impossible to develop wholesome traits without the proper knowledge to do so. Individuals must have the information

33

they need to flourish. In order for you to improve your way of living, you must commit to growing in knowledge. You can't expand beyond your level of knowledge. What you don't know can hinder your progress. You must obtain the right information that will help you develop in every area of your life. In the book of Hosea, God declares, "*My people are destroyed for lack of knowledge*" (**Hosea 4:6**).

Always keep a hunger for knowledge and wisdom. Once you begin to grow as an individual, things will start to change around you. Your perspective will change, and you'll begin to view problems and difficulties as opportunities. You now see life the way God sees it. It's called a Godly perspective. And when you see as God sees, you will act accordingly. God's greatest desire is for all of us to grow into the image of Christ (**Romans 8:29**). When we grow in Christ-like character, it's revealed in our conversations, attitudes, and conduct. Decide in your heart today that you will establish a growth plan for your life. Become a person of integrity who inspires and influences others.

Growth takes place only when you begin to walk out the knowledge you have obtained. You must practice what you've learned; otherwise, there will be no elevation. Knowledge attained without application is just gained information. It's not enough for us to just read and understand God's principles. We must become doers of these principles. When we place into practice the information we have learned, we'll start to see actual change and growth in our lives. Every opportunity you receive to apply truth to your situation is an opportunity for growth. When you do the right thing in spite of how you feel, you are developing as a person. It's not about feelings or emotions; it's about doing what you know to be true and allowing your emotions to catch up later.

Good qualities are developed when you decide to apply Biblical truths to your life. You might not recognize the growth immediately, but its occurring. Purification is taking place in the innermost parts of you. You are being transformed internally every time you apply God's principles to your problems or situations. The fruit of your obedience will eventually manifest in time.

We must be willing to remove everything and anybody that hinders our growth. If it's not helping you, it's hurting you. The people and things in your life that don't encourage growth will interfere with your progress. Remember, if you desire to move to the next level in your life, then you must develop good character. Start paying attention to how you react and respond to certain situations. This will give you an idea of what areas of your life that need improvement. Don't resist the process. Keep a desire to grow and always be willing to challenge yourself to shift to the next level.

Growing pains are associated with developing yourself. There is no growth without pain. I like to say, "No pain, No gain." There are flaws in your character that must be corrected. This will require you to give up some bad habits that have become a way of life for you. Giving up these habits will be difficult to do, but the pain is only temporary. The results that you acquire from this decision will be long-lasting.

There are some friends and relatives that you must detach yourself from to make progress. Now, this can be painful, but it's necessary. If they threaten your growth, then you must make the difficult decision to disconnect. These actions are essential for spiritual growth and development. This is the sacrifice you make when you are determined to build Godly character and grow to new heights.

As I indicated previously, it is vital for you to maintain good character. When you possess integrity and consistency, it works to your advantage and enhances your overall quality of life. Being a person of character simply means that you are honest, reliable, honorable, have integrity, courage, and are responsible. Maintaining these qualities will elevate you to new levels in every aspect of your life.

Remember, our growth is usually stagnated when we fail to develop in our thinking, attitudes, and actions. Most people will judge us by our conduct and behavior, which stems from who we are within; therefore, we must strive to be men of principle and women of integrity.

Questions for Discussion & Reflection:

1. What insight did you gain from reading this chapter as it relates to your Character?

2. Are you the same person in private and public? If not, in what areas?

3.   What is a hypocrite? Are there areas in your life that reflect hypocrisy? How can you make the necessary changes?

4. What voices are you allowing to speak into your life? Do they exemplify integrity and uprightness?

5. Does your character reflect the nature of God? What changes can you make to improve your overall character?

6. Write down the areas in your life that need to be developed. How will you start the growth process? What is your plan?

7. Identify the people in your life that is hindering your development process. What steps will you take to detach yourself from the individuals that are delaying your progression?

CHAPTER 3

SERVING WITH LOVE & HONOR

What is love? According to Merriam –Webster, love is "strong affections for another arising out of kinship or personal ties." In the Bible, there are several types of love mentioned which includes phileo love, eros love, storge love, and agape love. Phileo is the love that the city of Philadelphia was named after. This is where the term "brotherly love" derived from. Phileo is a love shared between friends, brothers, sisters, and other family members, but it is largely associated with a love that is shared between best friends. C.S. Lewis, a prolific Irish writer, and scholar states, "The friendship is the strong bond existing between people who share common values, interests, or activities." The biblical account of David and Jonathan is a great example of this type of brotherly bond. **1 Samuel 18:1-3** states:

> *"And it came to pass, when he had made an end of speaking unto Saul, that the soul of Jonathan was knit with the soul of David, and Jonathan loved him as his own soul. And Saul took him that day, and would let him go no*

more home to his father's house. Then Jonathan and David made a covenant, because he loved him as his own soul."

In this passage, we see where Jonathan loved David as himself. Love shared between best friends is exemplified in this relationship between Jonathan and David. Phileo love is not the passionate affection that usually exists between a husband and wife. Phileo love demonstrates a friendly type of interaction, much unlike Eros love.

Eros love is a Greek term that refers to a more passionate or sexual type of affection that usually exists between a husband and wife. As you probably can see, *Eros* is the root word for the English term erotic. In today's culture, the English translation "erotic" has become equivalent to a sexual lust which in turn gives it a bad name. The original intent of this love was to be shared between a husband and wife; however, society has perverted this sensual love. Eros is an intense and passionate type of love that sometimes can be unreasonable and damaging if practiced without contemplating the consequences. This is not a love that's usually common among relatives.

Storge love is more of a natural kind of love such as love between family members. This is the kind of love a parent and child have for one another and also a sister and brother. Because storge love is a natural love among family members, it's usually unavoidable and occurs unconsciously. This love can bond relatives, communities, colleagues, and social groups. Storge love is more of a physical expression of affection that stems from genuine motives and can be demonstrated with a hug, kiss, or other authentic expressions of love.

Phileo, eros, and storge are all different from the love described in the Bible that God commands believers to show among each other. This love is known as agape, which is similar to the love exemplified by Jesus when he sacrificed his life for humanity. The Greek word *agape* is frequently interpreted "love" in the Bible. "Agape Love" is an unconditional love that is unlike the three other types of love mentioned earlier. This kind of love is the noblest and generous love that there is. The core of agape love is benevolence, compassion, and generosity.

AGAPE LOVE

The most important love of them all is *agape* love, which is the God kind of love. According to Wikipedia, *agape,* is the highest form of love, the love of God for humankind. Agape is not similar to a brotherly love or a passionate love between a husband and wife. This is the kind of love that God has for us that was demonstrated by Jesus Christ on the cross. **John 3:16** states, *"For God so loved the world, that he gave his only begotten Son, that whosoever believeth in him should not perish, but have everlasting* *life*." Agape is a Godly love that is unselfish and unconditional; Often you will see this between a mother and child.

Agape is the love that God desires for us to show toward one another, and it's not based on feelings, emotions, or whether or not the person deserves it. Remember, it's unconditional love. The Bible explains that deeds and actions rather than feelings show agape love. Let's take a look at the biblical definition of love.   **1 Corinthians 13:4-7** defines love this way:

> *"Love suffers long and is kind; love does not envy; love does not parade itself, it is not puffed up; does not behave rudely, does not seek its own, is not provoked, thinks no evil; does not rejoice in iniquity, but rejoices in the truth; bears all things, believes all things, hopes all things, endures all things"*.

This scriptural reference speaks more about what love does rather than what it is. Let's dissect each of these definitions of love by starting with "love is patient and kind."

Are you long-suffering? If so, are you kind while you wait? Many of us may withstand for an extended period, but we are not patient and understanding while we do it. We usually tolerate our circumstances and situations because we have no other choice. For example, you might have someone you work with that continually offends you and disregards your feelings; however, when you refuse to retaliate and begin to display kindness despite their actions, you are exhibiting agape love. If you continue to demonstrate patience and kindness, whether a person deserves it or not, you will begin to experience growth in many areas of your life.

Love is not jealous nor does it envy others. Envy, as defined in Merriam-Webster's dictionary, is a feeling of unhappiness over another person's good fortune with a desire to have that same good fortune. It is impossible to love a person and envy them simultaneously. Envy is a feeling that is common to human nature, and unless we protect ourselves from it, it will cause a setback for us. One way to fight against feelings of jealousy and envy is to cultivate a desire to see others prosper. When you wish to see others blessed in life, those feelings of resentment will eventually eradicate over time. Learn to celebrate other people's victories and congratulate them on their successes in life. This will help you to eliminate any jealousy that's in your heart. Of course, this will not be easy, but as long as you make a conscious effort to practice blessing others, change is inevitable.

Agape is not a proud love. It is not conceited or self-centered. It looks out for the interest of others before its own. Proud is associated with the term "puffed up," which is a person that has an exaggerated opinion of their self. In the Bible, Paul states that a person should not "think of himself more highly than he ought" (**Rom 12:3**). We are to think soberly of ourselves, and have an accurate estimation of who we are. Vanity and pride can never cohabit with Godly love.

Godly love does not dishonor others. It is not rude, offensive, or disrespectful toward other people. As children of God, we ought to be polite, kind, and patient with one another. Refuse to dishonor anyone. People should be able to see God's love in your everyday life interactions. Be courteous, gracious, and honorable toward all individuals. This is the essence of Godly love.

The Bible instructs us to honor everyone (**1 Pet 2:17**). We must choose to respond appropriately when faced with difficult challenges in our life. Make choices that represent God's love and His Kingdom. This will not always be easy to do, but we must do it anyhow. We do what's right regardless of how we feel about it. It's not about our feelings; It's about walking in truth. A person that is offensive and ill-mannered toward others is viewed as a selfish individual that is only thinking of himself. And they have no consideration for others. Being concerned about the welfare of other people illustrates *agape* love, and it allows you to develop to higher levels in your personal and spiritual walk.

To grow and maintain our love walk, we must refrain from evil thinking. Developing will require you to cease from dwelling on negative thoughts. Please stop meditating on all the ways people have done you wrong or offended you. It's not mentally healthy. There will always be opportunities for people to hurt you or insult you; therefore, you must learn how to let things go and move forward. If not, this will be a stumbling block to your personal development.

I am inspired by one of the definitions of love in the bible that states, "…it keeps no record of being wronged" (**1 Cor 13:5**), which means we should avoid meditating and keeping count of the wrongs caused by others. Choosing to rehearse over and over in our minds the offenses and hurt brought on by other people will cause us to have thoughts of revenge and retaliation. If we continue to meditate on how we can "even the score", actions will eventually follow. Arnold Schwarzenegger, a well-known actor, and bodybuilder that served two terms as the Governor of California stated, "Where the mind goes the body will follow"; therefore, we must make a concerted effort to forgive others; otherwise, our love walk will be hindered.

When we choose to forgive, despite how we feel, we are maturing in ways that we don't necessarily realize at the time. Deciding to forgive someone is not about them as much as it is about you. Forgiveness allows you to release the emotional pain associated with past hurts. God's love is at work when you decide to forgive. Displaying respect and honor to people irrespective of their adverse actions and behaviors toward you is an indication of real growth. Once you make that decision to acquit others of the distress they may have caused you, God's Grace is released into your life, which in turn empowers you to walk in love the way God intended. Remember, forgiveness allows us to release the pain caused by others and the power it had over us.

Love withstands all things and endures all things. What does this mean? When you are filled with *agape* love, it will move you to protect, shield, and safeguard others. We all experience many different seasons in life that are not all delightful; however, love will bear up and assist others in their time of trouble. Other people cause some of the difficulties and afflictions we experience in life, but *agape* chooses to believe the best. Godly love is filled with faith and decides to look beyond the problems and focus on the potential that exists in every person.

For example, you have a friend that is always having problems or have done some things in the past that you perceive as distasteful, but you choose not to condemn them, and you remain hopeful. Agape love allows you to believe that this person can turn his/ her life around with the right support system and love. Now, of course, the person must have a desire to change; otherwise, it will never happen. But you can be an example to that friend of what love and support look like, which can significantly influence them and change their desires. You have more influence than you realize, so use it! Agape love believes the very best, regardless of what the situation may look like.

SELF-LOVE

Self-love is essential. You must love yourself; otherwise, loving others becomes an impossible task. Let me ask you a question. How do you perceive yourself? Do you view yourself the way God sees you? Or do you view yourself in light of your past mistakes and failures? In order to care for others in the manner that God instructs us to, we must love ourselves. One of the greatest commandments in the Bible teaches us to love God and love others as we love ourselves (**Matthew 22:37-39**). According to this verse, our love walk starts with loving God first, then loving ourselves the way He loves us. When we do this, we are now capable of sharing His love with others.

It is impossible to give out what you do not possess. If you have no love for yourself, you can't give any love. If you don't know how to receive mercy, you can't give mercy. Compassion must reside in your heart for you to love others the way God intends. When we treat people as well as we treat ourselves, this is equivalent to *"loving thy neighbor as thyself."*

Suppose you are at work and witness a Christian colleague losing his temper while speaking unpleasant and distasteful words. From that point forward, would you conclude that he is no longer a Christian or a possible hypocrite? Or would you display empathy for this person? Ask yourself this question: what would I desire for myself? There could have been many reasons why this Christian reacted the way he did. For example, it's possible that he was under severe stress from his home life, experiencing child problems, or even marital issues. We're not excusing his poor behavior; nonetheless, we should consider these events before making sudden judgments. I genuinely believe that we would desire for someone to give us the benefit of the doubt if we were in a similar situation; therefore, we must be mindful to treat others as we would like to be treated. When this becomes a common practice in your life, you're guaranteed to experience growth and elevation.

HONORING OTHERS

According to Baker's Evangelical Dictionary, honor "is to give weight or to grant a person a position of respect and even authority in one's life." When you honor someone, you are placing value on his or her life. It is a mark of respect. We are all made in the image of God according to Genesis 1:27; therefore, we should value everyone regardless of their color, creed, ethnicity, or background. God commands us to honor all people (**1 Pet 2:17**).

Some people make a conscious effort to dishonor others; however, this behavior is not pleasing to God and will ultimately hinder your growth. Honor should be your standard even if it's not the next person's standard. Maintain an attitude of respect, courtesy, and reverence toward others. Let honor be seen in your actions at home, work, school, church, and the shopping mall. Honoring others only with your words is not enough. Make sure you exhibit honor not only in your speech but also in your deeds. Father God, for example, is honored when we choose to obey His instructions and make choices that please Him. Managers are honored when employees do the work that has been assigned to them; parents are honored when their children submit to their rules. These are all actions and not just words.

ACCESS GRANTED

Honor is the culture of the Kingdom. You honor people whether you feel like it or not and whether you like them or not. God has called us to regard everyone. It's essential that you cultivate honor in your life because honor allows you access to the treasures and gifts that are stored on the inside of others. Let's say you been praying to God for wisdom on a matter and God places the answer to your prayers in someone that you dislike and dishonor. Well, you will miss your blessing because of your dishonor. God will always send our blessings through people. And sometimes He will send the answer to our prayers in packages that we're not fond of. That's why it's imperative to honor everyone.

When we value people for who they are, we're able to receive from them. Honor allows you access to the greatness in others. Remember, you will never receive the treasure God has placed on the inside of a person if you dishonor them. Respect one another; And when you do this, it allows you to unlock the gifts and treasures that God has placed on the inside of them. Honor pulls out the best in people. I remember hearing a great teacher by the name of Dr. Mike Murdock say, "Whatever you honor moves toward you and whatever you dishonor/disrespect moves away from you." You'll never be able to retrieve what you need from someone without honoring them. God has stored your blessing inside someone that's waiting for you to honor them, and you'll never receive it without honor. Honor should be our way of life.

HONOR GOD

According to the Bible, we should honor God in all that we do in life. This simply means we are to consider God before making key decisions, which is primarily viewing a situation through the eyes of God and acting accordingly. **Romans 14:8** says, *"If we live, we live to honor the Lord; and if we die, we die to honor the Lord. So, whether we live or die, we belong to the Lord."*

When we treat others with respect, we are honoring God. When we deem others as important, we are honoring God. When we treat others the way we would like to be treated, we are honoring God. Everything that we undertake in life should bring glory and high regard to God.

Another way we demonstrate reverence for God is through obedience. When we obey God's instructions, this communicates to Him that we worship and revere Him. God desires more than lip service from us. Some people honor God with their lips, but their hearts are far from Him (**Matthew 15:8**). Don't let this be you. Whatever you say, be willing to back it up with actions; otherwise, your words are useless. God is not impressed with our words. Our efforts are more of a concern to God because obedience is what causes us to mature and develop to the next level in life.

HONOR YOUR PARENTS

Honoring your parents is the first commandment with a promise in the Bible. It reads, "Honour thy father and thy mother: that thy days may be long…" (**Exodus 20:12**). Honoring your parents is a mark of respect and show high regard for their position. Your mother and father are life givers; therefore, they are worthy of your honor. Even if they were poor parents, they are still your mother and father. And God commands us to honor them. This applies to everyone, not just children. There is no age limit on respecting and revering your parents.

One way you can demonstrate to your children on how they should honor is by allowing them to observe you honoring and respecting your parents. Lead by example. Children will not do as you say, but they'll do as you do. Even when there are disagreements among you and your parents, you should still esteem their position as a parent. Perhaps your parents lived degrading lives, struggled with substance abuse, or even abandoned you. Whatever the situation may be, whether you believe they "deserve" honor or not, we should honor them anyway.

Although we are required to honor our parents, this does not mean we allow them to manage and control our lives as adults. It's unhealthy and also dysfunctional. Honoring your mother and father does not involve you doing things that are contrary to Godly standards. If a parent instructs you to do something that clearly opposes God's commands, then you must obey God rather than your parents (**Acts 5:29**).

HONORING AUTHORITY

Another group that we should express honor to is those who are in authority over us. God institutes all power; therefore, if we rebel against authority, we are rebelling against God. It is imperative that we respect the men and women that God has placed over us; otherwise, we are dishonoring Him. We're supposed to show regard for our supervisors, coaches, teachers, mentors, and other leaders. Even if we believe that they are incompetent or rude, we still must exercise humility by exhibiting honor to the people God has positioned over us. In **Romans 13:1-2** it says, *"Let every soul be subject to the governing authorities. For there is no authority except from God, and the authorities that exist are appointed by God. Therefore, whoever resists the authority resists the ordinance of God, and those who resist will bring judgment on themselves."*

When we practice the honor code, God will honor us. Dishonoring others is never pleasing to God. When you honor, God will exalt you to higher levels because of your obedience. For example, the Bible says, "...those who humble themselves will be exalted and those who exalt themselves will be humbled" (**Luke 14:11**). Once we start submitting to this principle and treasuring others whether they "deserve" it or not, we invite blessings and increase into our lives. Yielding to others is not easy and often requires an act of humility, but it's worth it. Don't block your blessings by dishonoring others. Honor brings rewards!

Questions for Discussion & Reflection:

1. What insight did you receive after reading this chapter?

2. Are you longsuffering toward others? Is your love toward others based on how you feel at that present moment?

3. Do you currently have thoughts of revenge and retaliation toward any individuals from your past? If so, how can you rectify this?

4. Are you happy about other people's accomplishments and good fortune? Or do you display jealousy?

5. Who have you celebrated or congratulated in recent months?

6. Do you walk in love and honor toward others? Or do you only honor the people that honor you?

7. Why should we honor others?

8. Do you treat people as you would like to be treated? Explain.

CHAPTER 4

WALKING IN HUMILITY

According to Merriam-Webster, humility is freedom from pride or arrogance, and the quality or state of being humble. It involves lowering yourself and being submissive at heart. An individual that is arrogant, prideful, haughty, or conceited lacks humility. When we choose to walk in humility, we are acknowledging our dependence on God. We recognize that every good and perfect gift comes from above (**James 1:17**). Meekness is not an indication of weakness; it's simply power under control. If you desire to be a follower of Christ, you must learn to walk in humility. It is vital to your faith walk.

Deciding to commit your life to God is the first step in developing a humble heart. Your attitude and responses to people and circumstances will begin to change once you learn how to view your experiences through the eyes of God. A person with a submissive heart refuses to look down on others and chooses to see the value in every human being.

For instance, a modest or meek woman that encounters someone that is less gifted or less fortunate than herself would not degrade that person or think more highly of herself. She would acknowledge that all human beings have value and are made in the image of God. Just because someone is less fortunate or disadvantaged, doesn't mean they deserve to be disgraced. People that dishonor others because of their social class or status do not possess a meek spirit. These individuals lack humility.

The Bible cautions us never to think we are better than we really are, but rather think of ourselves with sober judgment (**Rom 12:3**). Basically, be honest in your evaluation of yourself. Now, this doesn't mean you should demean or disgrace yourself. No, that's not what I'm saying. I'm merely insisting that we have a true estimation of who we are and realize that every human being has something to offer and contribute to society. Let's begin to think soberly about ourselves, and treat others with the dignity and respect they deserve as human beings. When we do this, it is an act of kindness that reflects the heart of God.

SPREAD KINDNESS

Humbleness is associated with gentleness and generosity. Humility is displayed when we extend kindness toward others. A submissive person will show affection toward others whether they deserve it or not. I've come to realize that a friend that's lowly at heart is more inclined to help you in a time of need than a prideful person. A humble individual is usually kindhearted and merciful; therefore, when you encounter someone that is self-absorbed and egotistical, this is a sign of a proud heart, and more than likely this person lacks compassion.

Jordan LaBouff, a psychologist at the University of Maine, writes, "Compassion is hard if you don't have humility." Approach each day with kindheartedness and look for ways to bring pleasure and joy to others. The Bible encourages us to be kind toward each other with love and genuine affection (**Rom. 12:10**). When you practice this type of behavior, you will begin to experience joy and growth throughout your life.

VALUE OTHERS

Make an effort to value everyone. Be willing to compliment others when deemed appropriate. It's always good to let the people in our lives know they matter to us. Everyone wants to feel that they are relevant, accepted, and respected by others. When we show others that they are significant and valued, we are exhibiting Christ-like characteristics. Strive to see the best in people and learn how to make allowances for each other's faults. This is the essence of humility.

There will always be someone that offends you intentionally or unintentionally because none of us are perfect. It is a part of the human experience. You will be hurt by someone at some point in your life. There is no way around it. Knowing this should prompt us to be more forgiving of transgressions

57

committed toward us. We all have faults of some kind; therefore, we should strive to understand a person's actions before we make judgments. **Colossians 3:13** says we should forgive and be tolerant with one another. Our desire to be forgiven by God should motivate us to forgive others all the same.

SERVING OTHERS

Serving others and meeting their needs shows your love and compassion for people. Our daily walk should consist of helping others, even when it's not convenient for us to do so. Always offer your best when presented with the opportunity to enhance someone else's situation. Think about how you would like to be treated. There are moments when we would appreciate someone helping us without expecting anything in return; therefore, we should offer the same. It really does require a submissive heart to serve and give freely with no expectations or no strings attached.

Our motives should always be to please God and not a person, knowing that our reward comes from Him. Everything we do should be to satisfy God (**Col. 3:23-24**). Make sure your expectations are in Him, rather than people. When you keep an open heart, you allow God to work through you to assist others and meet their needs. What a wonderful opportunity to be used by the Father!

TEACHABLE HEART

Do you have a teachable spirit? Having a teachable heart means your soul is open to receive correction and knowledge from others. A person that possesses this attribute is perfectly aware of their own limitations and willing to allow others to teach them. You must be inclined to change your viewpoints if they are not benefiting you. We can learn from anyone if we just maintain an open heart. Sometimes pride can prevent us from asking for help, direction, or advice when we really need it. Being receptive to others' experiences and knowledge can enhance our lives immensely.

When you don't allow others to pour into your life, it is a sign of pride. In the book Breaking Pride *by* Heather Bixler, she states, "Pride is often used as a way to protect our hearts and to hide the truth. Pride causes us to shut down and build walls." We can secure our hearts without creating barricades around it. Many of us have been hurt, abused, or disappointed in the past, which makes it difficult for us to open up; however, as we get closer to God, He will help us to overcome our fears. As we draw closer to God; He will draw closer to us (**James 4:8a**). Pride prevents us from walking in humility, and it impedes our growth process.

Are you able to take constructive criticism from other people? A person who's willing to be educated and corrected by others is considered wise. When you're ready to accept

59

constructive criticism, you will increase and expand to new levels. The Bible says, *"Give instruction to a wise man, and he will be yet wiser: teach a just man, and he will increase in learning"* (**Prov. 9:9**).

Admit to yourself any limitations and inabilities that you may have and seek out individuals that can assist you in these areas. Move out of your comfort zone, and refuse to take the road of least resistance. For you to grow, you must withstand opposition and endure trials. So, don't run from the challenges, embrace them. Be willing to challenge your old belief systems and open your heart to new ideas. Make sure you bless others by sharing the knowledge and wisdom that you have gained. These practices can transform your thinking and catapult you to higher levels.

SHOW GRATITUDE

In addition to maintaining a teachable heart, appreciate the life that God has given you. Be thankful for the good experiences as well as the bad. Don't waste your painful experiences because there is wisdom you can gain from your times of suffering. A person with a humble heart is thankful for every season in life. They recognize that their life experiences have shaped who they are today.

Be grateful for the gifts and talents that God has blessed you with to help others. Never hesitate to say "thank you" to friends, family, or strangers that show kindness and compassion towards you. When gratitude becomes a lifestyle for us, we will feel joy in the depth of our heart and souls. John F. Kennedy, the thirty-fifth President of the United States, quoted, "As we express our gratitude, we must never forget that the highest appreciation is not to utter words, but to live by them." In other words, maintain an attitude of gratitude that can be seen by others. By doing this, you are taking responsibility for your actions. Remember, it's about doing and not just saying.

TAKE RESPONSIBILITY

Accepting responsibility for your faults is the epitome of humility. You're acknowledging your mistakes and not blaming others when things go wrong in your life. I always like to say, "If you blame others for the bad things that happen, then you have to give them credit for all the good that transpires." Ultimately, it's your life, and you decide how much influence a person has over you.

Yes, others may contribute to some of your problems, but they don't have the power to control your reaction. You are in control of the way you respond to issues that arise in your life. Sometimes we need to look in the mirror and take ownership of the things that went wrong in our lives. Confessing and admitting our shortcomings empowers us to adjust and move forward. Then we'll begin to flourish and rise to higher dimensions. A person that covers their sins will not prosper, but if they confess the wrongdoings and reject them, they will receive mercy (**Prov. 28:13**). For you to advance to the next stage in life, you have to be honest with yourself; and be willing to address the areas in your life that need development.

Identify your shortcomings and trust that God's strength is made perfect in your weaknesses. He will supply the Grace you need to overcome any adversity in your life. God's power is demonstrated best in our insufficiencies (**2 Cor. 12:9-10**). When you are willing to admit that you need help and acknowledge that you don't have all the answers, it displays humility. God does his best work when we surrender and allow him to do what only He can do; otherwise, we will experience a life of pride and discontentment.

DESIRE CONTENTMENT

Concentrate on where you are in this season, and decide to be content whether you feel like you are thriving or not. Acknowledge that God has you exactly where he wants you to be at this time. The first-century writer Paul speaks about this in **Philippians 4:11-13,** which says,

> *"Not that I speak in regard to need, for I have learned in whatever state I am, to be content: I know how to be*

abased, and I know how to abound. Everywhere and in all things I have learned both to be full and to be hungry, both to abound and to suffer need. I can do all things through Christ who strengthens me."

Adversity comes only for a season. Do not be fretful, for circumstances are subject to change. Remain prayerful and accept that there are certain situations beyond your control. Releasing these concerns over to God will allow you to experience a more peaceful existence. Refuse to worry and be anxious about anything, but instead, pray about everything with a thankful heart and attitude. And when you do this, the peace of God which passes all understanding will guard your heart and mind (**Phil. 4:6-7**). Remain content in every season of your life. And remember, this requires faith.

FAITH AND HUMILITY

Our faith is ineffective without humility. It is in our humbleness that we truly please God. Faith and pride are opposite of one another; therefore, they are unable to coexist. Pride says, "I can manage on my own; I don't need any help." But faith expresses a need for God and trusts that He will intervene on our behalf to help us in our time of need. Faith says, "I need God to do for me what I cannot do for myself." Faith requires a dependency on God.

Humility is exemplified when we release our control over to God and trust that He has our best interest at heart. It's dangerous always to trust your own understanding because some things will transpire in your life that you will not understand. And that's okay. We don't know everything, and we shouldn't pretend that we do. It's a manifestation of pride. According to **James 4:6**, God opposes the proud, but gives grace to the humble. We must learn to trust God and be willing to submit to His plan in his timing. Stop trying to figure out everything and expect God to do what you cannot do on your own.

What are the areas in your life more difficult for you to trust God? As for me, my challenge was trusting God with my finances. I remember several years ago when my pastor taught a message on giving offering and tithes. Tithes represent ten percent of your weekly or monthly income. Tithing is a biblical principle that is taught in the Kingdom of God. When I first heard it, I was excited. But when the time came for me to actually do it, I was gripped with fear. For some reason, it was difficult for me to believe that I would be blessed if I contributed ten percent of my income to the House of God. I had faith in God for every other area of my life, but I struggled immensely in the area of finances.

Finally, I decided to trust God, despite the apprehension I felt. Later, I realized that everything I am and everything I own belongs to Him. God requires me to be a good steward over everything he has entrusted to me. We are called to be good managers over our finances, kids, homes, gifts, relationships, businesses, ministries, and other possessions. When I understood this, it liberated me and gave me the freedom to give of my finances without fear. I recognized that I don't own anything in this world, and I cannot take anything with me when I die. So, when I submitted to this principle of "tithing," it was the best decision I could have ever made. The more I gave, the more I received. My life hasn't been the same ever since. We have to trust God even when we lack understanding. **Proverbs 3:5-8** instructs us to:

> *"Trust in the Lord with all thine heart; and lean not unto thine own understanding. In all thy ways acknowledge him, and he shall direct thy paths. Be not wise in thine own eyes…"*

Living by faith requires us to depend on God. Faith believes without seeing. When you have confidence in God and rely on Him in every situation, you are walking in humility. As believers, we are required to walk humbly with God and follow the path that He has prepared for us. If we decide to take matters into our own hands, insisting that we can do it all ourselves, pride will develop in our hearts. Once this happens, we cannot walk in unity with God.

Humility will always lead to elevation. Therefore, if we humble ourselves under the mighty power of God, He will raise and elevate us in due time (**1 Peter 5:6**). Without humility, we are unable to grow spiritually and personally. Frederick Lenz, a renowned spiritual teacher of Buddhism, states, "Humility is the most important quality in the spiritual life. When it is lacking, spiritual growth stops." People who have a "know it all" mentality usually delay their development. Think about it. If you know it all, then there is no room for growth. Often-times we pride ourselves on what we know, not realizing there is so much more we don't know. I once heard a statement that says, "You don't know what you don't know." This is so true. We must remember that with lowliness of heart comes wisdom.

Wisdom is the by-product of humility; therefore, choose the way of wisdom. It's wiser to be humble (**Prov. 11:2**). Always be willing to humbly receive correction and constructive criticism when given. Your growth depends on it. Developing without correction and improvement is difficult. When you choose to accept correction, you will grow and be esteemed by God. God honors humility. Decide to demonstrate humility in your everyday interactions with others. And remember, humility always precedes honor (**Prov. 18:12**). Your humbleness will attract favor and honor to your life.

Allow God to give you honor and refuse to seek it for yourself. If you seek fame and glory for yourself, it usually leads you down the wrong path. Focus on esteeming others, and you will always receive honor in return. Look for ways to help others without wanting to know what's in it for you. This is a humble approach to life, which allows you to grow and serve others in the process. In Rick Warren's *The Purpose-Driven Life,* he states "humility is not thinking less of yourself, it's thinking of yourself less." A humble spirit is a Godly attribute that's extremely attractive and is guaranteed to yield amazing fruit in your life.

Questions for Discussion & Reflection:

1. What insight did you gain from reading this chapter as it relates to Humility?

2. Do you possess a humble attitude?

3. What are some ways you can bring joy and pleasure to others?

4. Do you serve others without expecting something in return?

5. What does it mean to have a teachable spirit? Are you always willing to learn from others? Can you accept constructive criticism?

6. How do you take responsibility for your faults and mistakes?

7. Do you trust God in every area of your life?

8. What are the areas in your life that are more difficult for you to trust God?

CHAPTER 5

A LIFE OF OBEDIENCE

Obedience is conduct that's considerate and attentive to laws and rules. It's your willingness to obey individuals that exercise authority over you. Biblical obedience means to hear, believe, submit, and conform to God's teachings. Obedience always requires a level of trust. Oftentimes people are not willing to submit to a law, principle, or other individuals if it requires effort and makes them uncomfortable. Also, they want to know that their obedience will yield good results. You might say, "How do I know obeying this principle will work?" Well, the reason a principle is guaranteed to work is that it's a law. Principles and laws will function regardless of your belief system. They will work in spite of how you feel about them.

For instance, the law of gravity will always work whether you believe it works or not. Let's say one day you decide to dive from the roof of a five-story building. More than likely you will collide with the ground and die. Gravity is a law, and your feelings and beliefs about this law will not change its effect. Once you receive a revelation of this truth, you'll begin to manage your life according to God's principles. His instructions will always produce good fruit if you obey them. When we know, understand, and conduct our lives according to these Godly principles, progress is inevitable.

OBEYING GOD

As followers of Christ, we are required to obey the laws of God. Now, please understand that God will not force us or pressure us to submit to His principles. We have to choose to obey. If we truly love God, then we shouldn't have a problem with submitting to his laws and conducting our lives according to his commands. Ask yourself, if I continuously disobey the teachings of God, do I really love him? Well, according to the Bible, you do not. **1 John 2:3-6** reads,

> *"And we can be sure that we know him if we obey his commandments. If someone claims, "I know God," but doesn't obey God's commandments, that person is a liar and is not living in the truth. But those who obey God's word truly show how completely they love him. That is how we know we are living in him. Those who say they live in God should live their lives as Jesus did."*

In other words, we can prove to God that we love Him by obeying his statutes. Our submission to God suggests that He is first place in our lives. When we observe His laws and precepts, it is a demonstration of respect and honor. It's not enough for us to say we love God, but it must be evident in our conduct. Actions will tell the real story.

Your actions will always be a good indicator of what you truly believe in your heart. Actions reveal your belief system. What you believe is evident in your works. Remember, your belief system will always dictate your behavior. That's why it's imperative that your belief system is based on truth. This reminds me of the phrase "Actions speak louder than words." What a true statement. People tend to believe your deeds more so than your words.

I find that often people speak and ramble on about their convictions, but their behavior is inconsistent with these beliefs. For example, I hear Christians claim, "I know that God is in control, and He's working on my behalf;" however, their actions seem to suggest otherwise. They often complain, grumble, worry and stress about situations that are beyond their control. Their actions are not consistent with their words.

If we truly believe that God is in control and that He is concerned about our lives, then we must not continuously stress about matters that are outside of our power. Yes, we may have some concerns, but we have to trust that God will help us to work through our dilemmas. Either you trust Him or not.

Place your confidence in God's abilities, and as a result, you will experience success in your day-to-day living.

Intentionally ignoring the principles and laws of God will result in a lack of growth and progression. You are exhibiting rebellious behavior when you purposely disregard God's directives. Rebellion is willfully disobeying the laws of this universe, which will eventually lead to a life of ruin and decline. When we decide to take matters into our own hands and invent rules along the way, we are essentially saying, "I know best, and my way is better." This type of thinking will eventually lead to destruction.

Just because your way of handling situations may seem right, that doesn't necessarily mean that it is right. In the book of Proverbs, it reads, *"There is a way which seemeth right unto a man, but the end thereof are the ways of death"* (**Proverbs 14:12**). This scripture is basically saying that there is a way that people think is true, but in the end, this road leads to destruction. These people lives are subject to ruin because they're leaning to their own understanding.

For instance, someone hurts you, and you say to yourself, "I do not forgive them, and I'm seeking revenge." Well, this method of thinking may seem justifiable and reasonable to you, but that doesn't make it right.

The correct response would be to let it go and not retaliate. Why is this? Because this is the approach that God instructs us to follow, which leads to freedom and elevation. It is not our job to punish people or take revenge. We are instructed to forgive and allow God to avenge us. *"Vengeance is mine says the Lord"* **(Rom. 12:19).**

The only way we're going to flourish in this life is by allowing God to vindicate us when others condemn us or wrongfully accuse us. Respond His way and not your way. And remember, your knowledge is limited. We don't always see things the way God sees them. Work on changing your perspective. Start viewing people and situations through the lens of God's grace. This will radically change your heart and attitude because now you see things from a Godly perspective.

If you have a desire to live a prosperous life, you must adopt God's way of thinking. Learn His thoughts and His ways. The Word of God is the mind of God. So, if we want to know the mind of God, we must study His Word. Check to make sure your decisions are in line with the principles of God. If not, I suggest you make better choices. Sometimes you may need to ask yourself, "What would Jesus do in this situation?"

Life is choice driven. And every decision you make will either help you or hurt you. Your choices in life will decide your future; so, choose wisely. Sometimes our lives don't seem to be functioning in the way we expected; however, we must continue to make the right choices and obey God despite how the situation looks. This is called walking by faith. And when you do this, it displays your trust in Him. We must realize that God doesn't command us to obey His instructions with the intentions of controlling us; it's to liberate us and free us. Obedience leads to freedom, but rebellion creates bondage. Operating your life within God's boundaries allows you to experience a life of blessings, liberty, and peace. **Deuteronomy 4:40** explains it to us this way,

> *"Thou shalt keep therefore his statutes, and his commandments, which I command thee this day, that it may go well with thee… and that thou mayest prolong thy days upon the earth, which the Lord thy God giveth thee, forever."*

This text is asserting that life will go so much better for us when we choose to follow God's principles. Our days on this earth will be extended. See, I don't know about you, but I desire to experience an orderly and peaceful existence. And this can only happen if I decide to reside within God's boundaries. God's only desire is to protect us from the potential harm and danger that occurs when we choose to operate outside of His laws.

BOUNDARIES

Boundaries are limits and cut off points that you incorporate into your life for protection. They create the necessary space between you and others. Proper boundaries assist us in keeping out the wrong people and influences. And once you have established these limits, there are certain activities and behaviors that you'll refuse to participate in; places you'll refuse to go and events you'll never attend because you have boundaries. When you have boundaries, the chances of you being improperly influenced is highly unlikely. You have set limits on what you will and will not do, and you are vocal about it. Maintaining proper boundaries allows you to avoid people and situations that may harmfully impact your life.

Having no restrictions in your life opens the door for trouble and chaos to enter. We can be kind and friendly, yet still, maintain boundaries. When you create borders and limits in your life, it doesn't mean you are keeping people away. However, if they are living destructively, then you must limit your interactions with them. If you don't, their destructive behavior will cause significant problems in your life. You don't want their reckless lifestyle to influence your character. Bad company will corrupt good character (**1 Cor 15:33**). God has instructed us to be kind and gentle without adopting the world's way of doing things. We must not conform to anything that's contrary to truth.

75

Setting boundaries imply that we are taking responsibility for our own lives. Each of us is responsible for the life God has given us. If your life is only reaping ruin and decay, you must only blame yourself. You are responsible for the choices and decisions you make daily. Blaming others for your wrong choices and lack of self-control merely displays negligence on your part. Be willing to acknowledge your faults, and learn from them. You will start to prosper in all areas of your life. Once you understand your shortcomings and begin to make the right adjustments, you'll need to start creating some boundaries for your life.

Implementing boundaries will protect you from those that lack self-control. The limits you set in place will not allow undisciplined people to do as they wish in your life. Remember, boundaries will protect you. They guard your life. The book of Proverbs teaches us that a man that has no rule or control over his own spirit is like a city that is broken down without walls (**Proverbs 25:28**). Your life must consist of borders and limits. Once again, this protects you.

If we choose to operate outside of God standards, we must accept the consequences that come along with those decisions. For every action, there is a reaction. You will always harvest what you plant; therefore, you should be mindful of the seeds you sow throughout your life. Plant seeds according to the future you envision. I always like to say, "If you don't want it in your life, don't sow it."

Wayne Dyer, an American philosopher, author, and motivational speaker, suggests, "Our lives are a sum total of the choices we have made." I can predict the quality of the choices you've made previously by observing your current life. Your life tells me everything I need to know. I tell people all the time that my life is a reflection of all the good and bad choices I've made. And if I want a different experience, then I must make different decisions and sow different type of seeds.

Please do not be deceived. We shall reap what we sow (**Gal. 6:7**). The law of sowing and reaping is always in effect whether you acknowledge it or not. Therefore, we must always consider the harvest of a decision before we act. Take a moment and think about the possible consequences and ask yourself, will this action reap good fruit or not.

When you decide to engage in specific endeavors, make sure you use wisdom. Participating in activities simply because they are trendy and popular is indeed not wise. Our standard of living should be based on Godly principles. I remember as a young child, I would say to my Mother, "Everyone else is doing it, so I want to do it." My mother would respond to me by saying, "If everyone else jumps off the bridge, will you jump as well?" Of course, my answer to this question was No", but my actions showed otherwise. Many of us today are following our peers because we want to fit in and be part of the group, but it's wiser to do the right thing and have fewer friends than to lower your standards and gain many friends.

My mother taught me a valuable lesson. I now understand that following the crowd could be detrimental to my future. Just because the majority is behaving in a particular manner does not suggest that it's right or beneficial for you. Sometimes it's easier to follow others, rather than to make unpopular decisions because you don't want to be viewed as the outcast. But different is good. Your growth and development demand that you make quality choices in your life.

Unpopular decisions tend to make us stand out, but that's okay. If the decision is beneficial for you and your family, then do it. Once you receive the revelation that being a follower of the crowd can be harmful to your future, you'll decide to obey God, despite what others say or think. Be a trailblazer. Discover your own path and refuse to be a follower. God created you to lead and influence others. His desire is for you to become who He has purposed you to be. And remember this, following God will always produce better results than following people. Your decision to do it God's way will inevitably lead to a prosperous and fulfilling life.

LIVING THE TRUTH

Your lifestyle is an indication of who and what you represent. Others can observe your life and determine whether you are living for God or yourself. Who are you representing? Your actions will speak for you. I like to say, "Let your walking do the talking." Our lifestyles will witness to others without us ever uttering a word. People can discern our convictions and beliefs based on our behaviors. Your life is a representation of your ideas and beliefs. You don't have to tell me what you believe; I see what you believe by observing your actions.

Live your truth. Proclaiming what you believe is not enough. Words tend to hold more weight when actions follow. When people observe that your words coincide with your lifestyle, they are more inclined to believe the things you speak. Just remember that when you fail to submit to divine principles, your life will never reflect your desired results.

Obey the truth. Practice what you preach. Make sure you walk out the knowledge that you've attained. Development can only be achieved through obedience, which is why we must apply God's teachings to our lives and not just hear them. Do you desire to live the blessed life? Well, this can only be accomplished by working the principles. The Bible instructs us to be doers of the truth and not just hearers **(James 1:22).** Words without actions are useless. When we hear the truth and fail to act on the truth, we are deceiving ourselves. Hearing without doing makes us a careless listener.

For example, let's say you look in the mirror one morning and notice that your face needs to be washed and cleansed. However, you decide to exit your home without properly washing your face. Deciding not to tend to your hygiene before leaving your house suggests that you were forgetful of what you observed in the mirror. This is the message that the writer is trying to convey in James 1:22. When you hear the truth and never walk it out, you are forgetful of the knowledge that you heard. We must be doers of the truth and refuse to be a careless listener.

Obeying the principles of God produces spiritual growth and wisdom. Wisdom is just applied knowledge. It's when you put the information you received to work. Wisdom is also making the right use of the knowledge you've gained. For us to shift to new levels in life, we must walk in wisdom and be willing to grow consistently. Development only comes when we are eager to put our faith into action. Trust the principles of God, and be prepared to step out on faith. Growth requires that you exercise your faith. Remember, faith without works is useless. **(James 2:17)**.

If we only believe and fail to do the work, we will not produce the harvest we desire. Works produce fruit. Since increase only occurs by exercising your beliefs, your territory will never be expanded based on faith alone. If you want God to enlarge your territory, you must be willing to get busy. No work, no increase. This is the truth, regardless of how you feel about it. Feelings will never change the truth.

Be careful not to allow your feelings to dictate your actions. Never make important decisions based on emotions alone. Your feelings should never override the truth. I always like to say, "Do what you know and not what you feel." Feelings are fickle, and they come and go. It's irresponsible of us to make decisions based on our mood at that moment. That's why it's vitally important for us to obtain the truth. Once we know the truth, we can apply it irrespective of our feelings. When you walk by faith despite what you see or feel, it transforms your life because you are no longer being distracted by what you see. Walking by faith demonstrates your trust in God's plan for your life. I believe when we follow His principles, and walk by faith and not by sight, we'll reap a desirable outcome at just the right time.

GOD'S TIMING

Be patient and willing to withstand the season, regardless of how long your breakthrough may take. Everything transpires in God's timing. When we respond to our circumstances the right way, we'll receive the right outcome. This outcome may not occur as swift as we would like, but it will happen. The Bible tells us that everything is perfect in its timing. There's a time and season for things to manifest. Once you get a revelation of this truth, you'll be more inclined to endure difficult and uncomfortable seasons. God knows the valuable lessons that can be gained from our challenging situations; therefore, He has no problem with extending a season. This testing season will grant you the valuable wisdom that will prepare you for future seasons and also propel you to the next level.

For example, there was a season in my life when I endured some significant difficulties with my supervisor. This was a very challenging and painful time for me. Based on my experiences, I viewed her to be unfair, unreasonable, and impossible to work with. I remember praying to God, saying, "Please relieve me of this situation." I needed God to assist me in finding new employment. I no longer desired to work with her. This was a very miserable season for me, and I just wanted it to be over. All the negative emotions that I felt were blamed on her, insisting that she was an evil individual. Even though the majority of my complaints were true, I failed to see my own faults. I continued to expose all of her flaws and weaknesses without regarding my own. Needless to say, the season was extended, and I understood why.

In this situation, there were valuable lessons that I needed to obtain if I was going to see the progression in my life. Self-examination was warranted. During this experience, I gained great insight about myself, which in turn allowed me to confront my issues and shortcomings. At that moment, I realized that it was more about me and my responses and not her. Regardless of her actions toward me, my response is what truly mattered. My reactions to her mistreatment would determine if I qualified to be advanced to the next stage of my life; therefore, I decided to respond according to God's principles. In doing this, I received a favorable outcome. The message I'm conveying is for you to focus on your own actions and live according to the truth. Always do the right thing and respond the right way, regardless of what the other person does. Changing another individual is impossible, but you can always improve yourself.

BENEFITS OF OBEDIENCE

When you decide to obey God's instructions, your life will be enhanced. You will experience a life of peace, joy, contentment, and spiritual growth. According to **Psalms 119:1-3:**

> *"Joyful are people of integrity, who follow the instructions of the Lord. Joyful are those who obey his laws and search for him with all their hearts. They do not compromise with evil, and they walk only in his paths."*

God covers and protects those who yield to His laws. Submitting to the truth will always reap blessings.

In the Bible, Jesus mentions that we are blessed if we hear the word of God and obey it (**Luke 11:28**). Blessings are always attached to obedience. Your prosperity is found in your obedience. Once truth becomes your lifestyle, others will be influenced and encouraged by you. Maintaining a life of obedience has the potential to motivate and inspire other people to uphold Godly standards. Your life, when submitted to God, becomes a witness to others without you uttering a word.

If you desire a greater connection with God, begin to obey Him. Do what he instructs you to do. The more you follow him, the more intimate the relationship becomes. Our relationship with God grows deeper because of our submission to His precepts. When you submit your life to God, it is a reflection of your faith and trust in the King. God is faithful to his Word, and He will continually respond to our act of obedience toward Him. Always remember that the promises of God are attached to your willingness to obey Him. Conduct your life according to the pattern of God, and you'll reap many benefits in this life and future generations.

Faithfulness is the key. Continue to be faithful and obedient to God's principles. Your obedience will unlock doors to prosperity, increase, and the enjoyments of life. In the book of Job, it reads, "If they obey and serve him, they shall spend their days in prosperity, and their years in pleasures" (**Job 36:11**).

Questions for Discussion & Reflection:

1. After reading this chapter, what insight did you gain as it relates to Obedience to God?

2. Do you struggle with obeying God? If so, in what areas and why?

3. Does your conduct exemplify God's nature and character?

4. What are boundaries? Do you maintain boundaries in all of your relationships? If so, list two boundaries you have set.

5. Define wisdom. How does wisdom help your life shift to the next level?

6. What season of life are you currently in? What lessons have you learned from past seasons that are helping you in this current season?

Next Level Living

CHAPTER 6

THE BLESSED ATTITUDES

Maintaining the right attitude is the key to living a life of peace, love, and abundance. When your attitude reflects the character of Christ, you invite blessings into your life. God's blessings are promised to us when our approach to life aligns with the nature of God. As believers, we should strive to present a Christ-like attitude at all times.

Blessed are the individuals who maintain Godly mindsets and conduct their lives according to Godly principles. These kinds of people refuse to conform to society's philosophies about life. A worldly pursuit of happiness is not the way to divine blessings. Majority of people seek happiness in riches, material wealth, titles, leisure, and positions; however, these things only provide temporary satisfaction. The blessings of God offer you peace, contentment, joy, and fulfillment.

In the Bible, Jesus is recorded teaching "The Beatitudes," which are considered the "blessed attitudes" that we should embody. **Matt 5:3-11** reads:

"Blessed are the poor in spirit: for theirs is the kingdom of heaven. Blessed are they that mourn: for they shall be comforted. Blessed are the meek: for they shall inherit the earth. Blessed are they which do hunger and thirst after righteousness: for they shall be filled. Blessed are the merciful: for they shall obtain mercy. Blessed are the pure in heart: for they shall see God. Blessed are the peacemakers: for they shall be called the children of God. Blessed are they which are persecuted for righteousness' sake: for theirs is the kingdom of heaven. Blessed are ye, when men shall revile you, and persecute you, and shall say all manner of evil against you falsely, for my sake."

According to the Strong's Greek Dictionary, the word "Blessed" means "happy, fortunate, and prosperous." It is God's desire for us to live a blessed and abundant life, which can only be found through a relationship with Him. Jesus proclaims, "...I c*ome that they might have life, and that they might have it more abundantly* (**John 10:10**)." There is no abundant life without us possessing the right attitude. Let's look at some attitudes that we must develop to receive the divine blessings.

POOR IN SPIRIT

Being "poor in spirit" is an attitude of humility that we all must possess to receive divine favor in our lives. "Poor in spirit" just means we should maintain a humble attitude recognizing our need for divine guidance. It's when we realize that we are dependent on God and that we're spiritually empty, destitute, and deprived without Him. For us to maintain this attitude, we must lower our egos and have a true estimation of ourselves. In other words, try not to think you are better than you really are. Be honest and clear-headed in your evaluation of yourself (**Romans 12:3**).

We must understand that everything good in our lives is a gift from God. It is because of His grace that we can accomplish all that we do. Being poor in spirit is placing our lives in God's hands and trusting Him to guide us along the right path. When you do this, you can't go wrong because God will never fail you. I need you to trust Him. God has your best interest at heart.

The opposite of "poor in spirit" is to have a proud and arrogant heart. If we are not careful, it's easy for us to allow our education, accomplishments, social status, hard work, and deeds to inflate our egos. It's okay for us to feel good about our achievements if we understand where our real source of strength and ability comes from. God is our source, and when we maintain an arrogant and self-righteous attitude, it hinders us from seeking Him and relying on Him more.

When you solely depend on your own ability and strength, it will inevitably lead you down the wrong path because you are operating in pride. According to **Proverbs 16:18**, *"Pride goeth before destruction, and a haughty spirit before a fall."* We were built to need God. And if you maintain that proud spirit, thinking you can survive life on your own, you will eventually experience much sorrow and heartache in your life. Remember, God desires to help us, and honestly, we need His help whether we realize it or not. God has plans for us that far exceed any plan that we can ever imagine for our own lives. Remain humble and allow Him to lead you down the right path.

THOSE THAT MOURN

Jesus asserts, *"Blessed are they that mourn, for they shall be comforted"* (**Matthew 5:4**). In this text, mourn means to grieve and be sad. Why does Jesus say we are blessed when we are sad or grieving? In this verse, Jesus is placing value on sadness, and He's informing us that sorrow will produce blessings. Mourning our sin is an indication that we are in tune with our need for God's healing and forgiveness. When we look at the condition of our lives without Christ, this should bring about a sense of sadness that ultimately leads to a pursuit of God. Only those who pursue God for healing and restoration truly recognize their need for Him and mourn their iniquities.

Think about your past regrets, losses, and brokenness that changed your attitude about God and life. Sometimes when I think about my past mistakes and wrongdoings, it causes a feeling of regret. But then I realize that God has forgiven me; this brings comfort and great joy to my heart.

True mourning is regretting past sins, transgressions, and time wasted on ungodly things. Mourning these past indiscretions should result in you seeking change and wholeness in your life. It's time for you to change your perspective about some things, turn away from your past, and decide to move forward to new beginnings. We are consoled and blessed by God when we do this. When we receive God's forgiveness of our past vices, it allows His love to flow into our hearts, which removes the shame and the guilt. Once the guilt is removed, we can experience God's compassion and peace. And this produces a humble and meek heart.

MEEKNESS

There was a time in my life when I believed that meekness was a sign of weakness, and I'm sure you did too. But that's not true. Meekness does not suggest weakness. It is power under control. The Biblical meaning of meekness implies lowliness, respect, and patience. A person that embodies meekness is humble, teachable, submissive, tolerant, and gentle. Do you embody these qualities?

Walking in meekness and humility requires strength. For example, if someone at your job offends you, and you have the power to retaliate, but instead, you decide to use your authority to benefit them, you are demonstrating meekness. Charles Wesley, a notable Evangelist and English leader of the Methodist movement, stated, "The person who bears and suffers evils with meekness and silence is the sum of a Christian man." If you are a person that's easily provoked, easily angered, and you often lose control, then you may not be meek at heart. In the Bible, Jesus defines himself as being "meek and lowly in heart." This is what we should strive to become daily. When we treat others with care and refuse to seek revenge or repay evil with evil, it exemplifies a submissive heart. And this is the kind of heart Jesus possessed.

For example, the Bible explains to us how Christ was tortured, insulted, wounded, and persecuted, yet he never fought back. He had the authority and the power to harm and destroy the religious leaders that were persecuting Him, but instead, He trusted the justice of God. *"He did not retaliate when he was insulted, nor threaten revenge when he suffered. He left his case in the hands of God, who always judges fairly"* (**1 Peter 2:23**).

Jesus endured the suffering bestowed upon him by His perpetrators and pleaded to God for their forgiveness. He petitioned God by saying, *"Father, forgive them, because they do not know what they do…"* (**Luke 23:34**). This is the epitome of meekness. Can you forgive the individuals that persecuted you, lied on you, gossiped about you, or hurt you? If you desire to maintain a submissive attitude, you must learn to forgive and let go. Our goal should be to imitate Christ because He is our model. I want to challenge you to love like Christ, forgive like Christ, and show compassion like Christ. When you do this, you'll begin to cultivate a new heart. Remember, when you are seeking God and striving to be Christ-like, it will allow you to experience a blessed life. Always keep that hunger and thirst for God's truth.

HUNGER AND THIRST FOR RIGHTEOUSNESS

According to scripture, "*Blessed are those who hunger and thirst for righteousness, for they shall be satisfied*" (**Matt 5:6**). Jesus is saying that our appetites will be filled when we hunger for His truth. Also, this text implies that our lives are blessed when we continuously strive to improve ourselves. We should constantly be evolving and aiming to be better, greater, and more Christ-like. Being content with your current spiritual condition is unacceptable. There's still room for improvement. Be willing to grow and change. Change can be good for you, and everyone that's connected to you. As for me, I'm always seeking to go higher and to shift to new dimensions in my thinking and my life.

When we hunger and thirst after Godliness, we are guaranteed to be filled because God's desire is for us to develop and move to the next level. He doesn't want you to stay stuck. But you have to crave and have a hunger for growth. If you don't have a desire to grow, then you won't grow. Your passion for knowledge and change will allow you to develop in every aspect of your life. The more truth we know, the more we are set free. You can't do more if you don't learn more. Continue to seek knowledge. Become a lifetime learner and keep an appetite for wisdom. When you are challenged with adversity, this is the time to properly apply the knowledge you've learned. And when you do this, you will start to see progress and growth in your life. For example, let's say there is a problem at the workplace, and you desire to handle this situation in a Godly manner. So, you begin to seek Godly wisdom on how to resolve this conflict. This pursuit of knowledge is a prime example of what it means to hunger and thirst after righteousness.

When we're confronted with difficult situations, we must learn to seek God's wisdom first. Please avoid taking matters into your own hands because that usually results in chaos, strife, and discord. Bad decisions produce negative consequences. Sometimes our decisions are just based on the wrong information. I believe that knowledge is power, and for us to make better decisions, we need new information. If you change what you know, you change your life.

When you yearn for knowledge and wisdom, you will eventually start making better choices in your life. Remember, wisdom is key. It affects your relationship with God and other people. If you have a right relationship with God, it should influence your relationships with family, associates, friends, and colleagues. I see many people who say they have a great relationship with God, but they fail in their relationships with others. Honestly, I question their relationship with God. I don't believe you can be close to God and not become like Him. And when you become like God, you interact with others like Him. The closer you are to God, the better your relationships will be with others. Great relationships require a level of compassion and mercy. These are Godly attributes that we must possess to maintain healthy, long-lasting relationships. I choose to give mercy because God is merciful towards me.

BLESSED ARE THE MERCIFUL

Mercy is when you exercise kindness and empathy toward other people. God is merciful towards us. And I'm pretty sure that all of us have experienced His tenderhearted love and care. There have been times in my life when I made some pretty bad decisions, and God didn't allow me to receive the full punishment that I deserved. God extended His love and mercy towards me.

See, God knows about all of our transgressions, yet He is still willing to show compassion toward us on a daily basis. And we are obligated to do the same toward our fellow man.

God commands us to treat others like we would like to be treated. You want mercy, give mercy. The more you bestow mercy to others, the more you will receive. It's called sowing and reaping. Sowing and reaping is a spiritual law that operates in our lives whether we agree with it or not. And anytime you break the law, there are built-in consequences. You will always harvest what you plant in life; therefore, when you sow bad seeds, there are consequences attached. But remember, God is merciful. If we make mistakes, and we will, God is willing to show us mercy to prevent us from receiving the full punishment. He is a merciful God!

In the Bible, Jesus declares that we are blessed when we are merciful toward others. He says, *"Blessed are the merciful: for they shall obtain mercy"* (**Matthew 5:7).** I challenge you to show compassion for other individuals whether they deserve it or not. I realize that our basic nature rebels against this concept. We're more prone to grant mercy when we think someone deserves it, which is a sign of self-centeredness. Stop making decisions based on how you feel at the moment, and decide to do the right thing regardless of how you feel. Remember, feelings are fickle. They change all the time.

Our decision to show compassion and empathy toward other people should be based on God's truth and not our emotions. Truth must always supersede and override what you feel in the present moment. Always act on what you know, and not on how you feel. Follow the truth. Cultivate God's principles in your heart and watch how your life starts to change for the better. Everything we learn must be developed in the heart first before it can affect our lives and the people we encounter.

PURE IN HEART

Having the right motives is more important than performing good deeds. If the motive is wrong, the deed is wrong. Sometimes we can misjudge people by only focusing on their behavior. Many people do the right things for the wrong reasons. They are doing good things with an impure heart. Sometimes I question people's motives. Not that I'm paranoid, I just desire to know the condition of their heart. Why are they doing what they do? Is there a hidden agenda? Remember, God sees everything. He knows the true motive behind our actions. As humans, we tend to look at the outward appearance, but God always observes the heart **(1 Samuel 16:7)**.

Strive to maintain a pure and clean heart. It's attractive. People gravitate to individuals with pure hearts. There is something sweet and refreshing about a person with a clean heart.

A pure heart is a heart that's uncontaminated, genuine, refined, and real. I desire to have this kind of heart. That's why I try always to check my motives before I agree to perform a deed or service. It's my way of making sure my heart is in the right place. We know countless people that perform deeds with ulterior motives. And the only way to detect whether a person's actions are coming from a genuine place is by continuous observation. Pay attention to their responses and reactions in challenging situations. Whatever behavior a person consistently displays in different settings is their true character.

The Bible explains to us that we discern a person's heart by their fruit. In this case, fruit represents actions. You will know the true nature of a person by the fruit they bear (**Matthew 7:16**). Are they critical, condemning, and judgmental? Or are they loving, kind, and compassionate? What type of fruit do they bear? Watch their conduct. If they display the same behavior, over and over again, then you can accurately discern the condition of their heart. Make sure their conduct is in agreement with their words. If a person's behavior is not consistent with their verbal communication, then their words are useless. Your words carry no weight if your actions are not in agreement. It all starts with your thinking.

Strive to think pure thoughts. When impure thoughts arise, replace them with God's truth. I've learned that when you meditate on the wrong ideas, you will eventually harvest wrong behavior. Where the mind goes, the person eventually follows. Your body will always follow the thoughts you choose to keep and meditate on. Therefore, if you don't want something in your life, stop thinking about it. Did you know that the condition of your heart affects your relationship with God? *"Blessed are the pure in heart; for they shall see God"* (**Matt. 5:8**). Our ability to know God on a deeper level is predicated on the purity of our hearts.

Individuals that possess a pure heart are usually transparent, and they have an intense desire to please God. These kinds of people have surrendered their life to God. If we desire to live a surrendered life, we must invite God into our hearts and allow Him to cleanse us. God is the only one who can purify our hearts and make us new. Doing this on your own is impossible. The Spirit of God is the one who transforms your heart; however, the transformation process will require your approval and cooperation. The Spirit of God will not force us to change our hearts. We must be willing to submit to the process and do our part as well. Your daily prayer should be, *"Create in me a clean heart, O God; and renew a right spirit within me"* (**Psalms 51:10**). Surrender and allow God to renovate your heart so that you can experience an enjoyable life filled with peace and tranquility.

PEACEMAKERS

Are you at peace in your life? Have you made peace with your past? There is no real peace without the presence of God in your life. He is the Prince of Peace, and when we allow Him to use us as instruments of peace, we are called the children of God. The Bible declares, *"Blessed are the peacemakers: for they shall be called the children of God"* (**Matthew 5:9**).

In order to present peace to others, you must first possess inner peace. It's impossible to be peaceable when you have inner turmoil and conflict. A person with no inner peace tends to sow strife, discord, division, and disharmony among others. This reminds me of the phrase "misery loves company," which means a person who's miserable and lacking peace desires to see other people miserable as well. This is disturbing to me. I've heard people say, "since I don't have peace, I don't want anyone around me to have peace either." Shame on you if this is your mindset. This kind of thinking is selfish and destructive. And I'm sure we can all say that we've met people like this. More than we care to remember.

Just because your life is disorderly and chaotic doesn't mean you should desire the same for others. Learn from people who seem to have an abundance of peace in their lives. Ask them about their lifestyle. Observe what they do daily and start incorporating some of the same principles into your own life. God instructs us to pursue peace at all cost. Walk in unity with others, and refuse to sow discord and strife. Make it your goal to depart from evil and strive to do good; seek peace, and pursue it (**Psalms 34:14**).

The first step to restoring your peace is building an intimate relationship with God. He is the source of your peace and happiness. Whatever is stirring in your soul— whether it be offenses and hurts from the past or abuse— make peace with it. Allow God to restore you through healing and deliverance cf the painful wounds inflicted by yourself or other people. Once we surrender these hurts and pains to God, we are permitting Him to replenish our souls so that we can be an instrument of peace for the Kingdom of God.

If we desire to live a peaceful existence, we must be willing to endure the healing process. I always like to say, "You can't give something you do not have." If your soul is deficient of peace and serenity, then you're unable to offer that to others. Peace is cultivated from the inside out; therefore, once you've made peace internally, it will radiate outwardly.

Do you want to experience the blessed life? Start seeking healing and restoration, and watch how you begin to experience peace in your heart. Maintaining harmony with difficult people in difficult circumstances can be challenging. But do it anyway. Decide to sow peace on purpose, despite how you feel. It's not easy to spread peace in a season of persecution and mistreatment, but you can do it. God would never ask us to do something we were incapable of doing.

PERSECUTION

When you are persecuted for righteousness sake, consider yourself blessed. What does this mean? When people come up against you, condemn you, or try to hurt you because you do the right thing, you are considered blessed according to **Matthew 5:10** which states, *"Blessed are they which are persecuted for righteousness' sake: for theirs is the kingdom of heaven."* If you are a follower of Christ, you will attract persecution and opposition. There's no way around it. People are going to berate, harass, criticize, and taunt you. It comes with the territory; therefore, you must continue to do good works and declare that you are blessed. Remember, this is what we signed up for when we decided to live a Christ-centered life. But it's all worth it. There is no life outside of God.

Many people will misunderstand you just as they did when Jesus walked the earth. The Bible records Jesus' words in **John 15:18**, *"If the world hates you, know that it hated me before it hated you."* You are not exempt; however, God is always with you during these challenging seasons. He's strengthening you, and helping you to overcome all adversity. If we just stick with it, there is something great in store for us. We will be blessed beyond measure.

Keep the right attitude in every situation. In doing this, your outlook and behavior will begin to reflect the nature of God. You will eventually walk in divine favor, influencing others everywhere you go. People are always watching. They are seeking the truth, whether they admit it or not. Our goal should be to inspire and motivate people to live Christ-centered lives. Remember, attitude is everything. Maintain the right attitude because it's impossible to grow and inspire others with the wrong mindset. When we have the right outlook, we'll continue to develop and shift to new levels in our lives. And when we grow, we can help others to grow as well.

Questions for Discussion & Reflection:

1. After reading this chapter, what insight did you gain as it relates to blessings and maintaining the right attitude?

2. What does it mean to be blessed?

3. Define meekness. Do you embody this Godly trait?

4. Do you have a hunger and thirst for truth? What changes are you willing to make in order to grow in God?

5. Are you merciful? Do you have compassion for others regardless of how they treat you? Please explain.

6. What does it mean to be pure in heart? What steps can you take to improve in this area?

CHAPTER 7

FORGIVENESS: LET IT GO

Forgiveness is the act of releasing an offender of any wrong or hurt they may have caused you, whether they deserve it or not. It is a decision to let go of resentment or vengeance towards a person or group of people. When we choose to forgive, we're wiping the slate clean, canceling a debt, or as I love to say, "Letting it go." In the Bible, the Greek word for forgiveness means to "let it go."

Forgiveness is a concept that's easier said than done. Majority of people find it very difficult to let go of offenses and hurts caused by others. I really do believe that most of us desire to let it go, but we lack the knowledge of how to do it. For some reason, we feel we are letting the offender off the hook, but we're not. This is about our freedom; therefore, we must make up in our minds that we're going to forgive the people that have offended us, whether we feel like doing it or not. It's a process, and it can be a painful process, but your freedom is worth it. We are instructed by God to maintain an attitude of forgiveness.

The act of forgiveness is taught throughout the Bible as a way of living. I suggest that you learn how to forgive quickly so that you're able to move forward in your life. Holding on to unforgiveness is a heavy burden that you don't want to carry around. In the book of Luke, Jesus says we should pray that our sins are forgiven as we forgive anyone who is indebted to us. We must cancel their debt. This is a command by God, not a suggestion. If we refuse to forgive others of their faults and transgressions, why should we expect God to forgive us of our wrongdoings? When we grant forgiveness to others, we'll harvest forgiveness in return. People will be more prone to forgive us. Why? Because you always reap what you sow. It's a spiritual law that's still in operation, whether we realize it or not.

Majority of people who offend or hurt others desire to be forgiven, yet they wrestle with this concept when they are the wounded. Why is this? Well, I believe it's easier to want mercy than to give mercy. You see, there a lot of things we want from others that we're not willing to give. And it shouldn't be this way. If you desire forgiveness, be ready to extend the same to others. **Matthew 6:14-15** advises, *"For if ye forgive men their trespasses, your heavenly Father will also forgive you: But if ye forgive not men their trespasses, neither will your Father forgive your trespasses."* You must learn how to "let it go" if you expect to receive mercy in return.

LET GO

It is impossible for us to live in this world and never be offended, hurt, misunderstood, or rejected. It's guaranteed to happen at some point in our lives. That's why it's critical that we grasp this concept of forgiveness if we desire to live a peaceful and stress-free life. Stress is associated with not forgiving. According to the Journal of Health Psychology, not forgiving others can cause stress, which eventually takes a toll on your mental health over time. The longer you retain bitterness, resentment, and anger in your heart, the more likely you are to experience a decline in your mental and physical health. It's all connected.

Dr. Steven Standiford, Chief of Surgery at the Cancer Treatment Centers of America, says that unforgiveness can make people sick. Emotional wounds are more harmful to our health than we realize. Built up anger will weaken our immune systems, causing us to feel sick more often. For this reason, we must make forgiveness a lifestyle rather than a one-time event. We must learn how to surrender the burden of anger and resentment over to God, and allow Him to heal the wounds caused by others. When we forgive from our hearts, we will begin to experience the peace of God in our souls. Unforgiveness is an unnecessary burden that we carry around, not realizing that it weighs us down, make us sick, and hinders our growth.

It's very difficult to move forward in life when you are burdened with anger and bitterness. When you decide not to forgive, it alters your perspective, and in turn, influences your responses and decisions in life. For example, a person who's been carrying around bitterness for years will be inclined to examine the motives and actions of others through the lenses of "unforgiveness." Because they haven't forgiven their offenders, they tend to be paranoid and suspicious of other peoples' intentions. This behavior will cause you to lose friends and even prevent you from making new ones. So, stop harboring ill-will toward other people. It's not hurting them; it's only hurting you.

Holding on to hurts and pains of the past will affect other aspects of your life, such as your relationship with family, friends, and colleagues. If you refuse to resolve your troublesome issues from the past, you'll bring that hurt into every new relationship and new experience. Not forgiving will prevent you from enjoying yourself and connecting with other people. When you are consumed with thoughts of anger and resentment, it robs you of the present moment and produces feelings of depression and anxiety. That's why it's imperative that you confront these issues, and allow God to help heal you. It's time to be set free!

FREEDOM

The first step to becoming free from bitterness is you being honest about the condition of your heart. You cannot correct what you don't confront. Admit that you are hurt and angry with the person or group of people who offended you. Deal with your feelings and reject the urge to suppress those emotions. We must pray to God for strength through this process. His grace will help us to work through these overwhelming feelings.

Depending on the level of offense, it can be impossible to forgive in your own strength. This reminds me of the scripture where Jesus insists, *"Without me, you can do nothing"* (**John 15:5**). I wholeheartedly agree with this verse. We need the grace of God to empower us to release these people of the pain they have inflicted upon us. Sometimes the hurt is too deep, and the pain is too intense to resolve it on our own. The good news is that God will give us the grace we need to let it go.

Yes, God is willing to help us become free from the bondage of offense; however, we must be willing to do our part. For instance, you have to stop rehearsing and meditating on the wrongs that were done to you. It's time to change your way of thinking; this is within your control. God is unable to deliver us without our cooperation, and we are unable to be healed and restored without God. Once again, we're not freed by our own strength, but by the Power of God. According to **Zechariah 4:6**, we will overcome— not by our might, nor by willpower—but by His spirit. We must allow God's love to flow through our hearts. His love and grace are sufficient. It's enough! Allow God to help you to overcome the hurt and pain that resides in your soul.

God would never instruct us to do something without granting us the power to do it. That would be unfair. And since we know He has instructed us to have mercy on others; He has empowered us to obey His command. You have the power to forgive, so just do it. Start the process today and be committed to change. And remember, your journey of forgiveness consists of you forgiving yourself as well.

FORGIVING YOURSELF

God forgives our transgressions; therefore, we should forgive ourselves. *"If we confess our sins, he is faithful and just to forgive us our sins, and to cleanse us from all unrighteousness"* (**1 John 1:9**). Be honest about your wrongdoings and be willing to acknowledge your faults. It keeps you accountable. How can you heal from something that you don't acknowledge? Avoid justifying and excusing bad behavior and admit when you're wrong. When you do this, it keeps your heart pure. It also keeps your relationship with God in right standing.

What does it benefit you to hold on and wallow in guilt and condemnation? Doing this only causes you to be withdrawn and critical of yourself and others. It's not just about you. Did you know that when you fail to forgive yourself, it affects all of your relationships and the people you are connected to? For example, if you're miserable and very critical of yourself, you tend to project those feelings on the people closest to you, such as your spouse, your children, your parents, your friends, and colleagues. This is not fair to them. They shouldn't have to suffer because you refuse to deal with your issues.

Sometimes it's much harder to forgive others when you do not forgive yourself. You tend to treat people the way you treat yourself. We must face what we've done in the past and deal with it so we can move forward. When you decide to forgive yourself and keep moving ahead, it doesn't imply that you're excusing your past behavior; however, you are simply accepting what happened and choosing to move on. What's done is done. There is no changing the past. If we fail to forgive our past mistakes, we will never experience the breakthrough that God desires for us. How can you move forward and help others if you're constantly beating yourself up over past failures and mistakes? I've come to realize that when we condemn ourselves, it only produces feelings of worthlessness, shamefulness, and hopelessness. It's not worth it.

Oftentimes, we believe God is condemning us, but we are condemning ourselves. God doesn't condemn us; He convicts us. According to **Romans 8:1**, *"There is no condemnation to them which are in Christ Jesus..."* God convicts us of His righteousness. He reminds us of His principles and how to apply them to our situations. Majority of us find it difficult to forgive ourselves for things like hurting someone else, failing in our marriages, not doing something we should have done, and self -destructive behavior. But we must realize that we are not unique in our sufferings. There are others all around the world who are experiencing similar situations. If they overcame, so can we. When you realize that you're not alone, it gives you hope and a sense of confidence that you can be healed as well.

NOT A VICTIM

Refuse to view yourself as a victim. Even though you may have been victimized, you are not a helpless, powerless person who can't recover. It's your decision. You can decide to stay a victim or embrace the mindset of a conqueror. Combat those oppressive thoughts, and choose to forgive the person or group of people who offended you. When forgiveness becomes valuable and important to you, you will begin to initiate change. Our lives are affected mentally and physically when we refuse to forgive and let go. Reflect on the things that have hurt you, and decide to release it today. Take back your power.

The people that hurt you retain power over you when refuse to forgive them. For instance, let's say your colleague has offended you, and every time they enter your office or show up at a staff meeting, your disposition changes. Their presence alters your attitude, and you become angry and irritated when you see them. This is a problem. They have too much power over you. If the person who offended you can enter the same room as you and dictate your mood and attitude, they are exercising control over you whether you believe it or not. This power is unconsciously granted to the offender when you refuse to let go of the offense.

I once heard a phrase that says, "Holding on to unforgiveness is like drinking poison, wishing the other person would die." For some reason, we believe that not forgiving a person is hurting them or causing them pain. Not true. We are only hurting ourselves when we fail to forgive someone. More than likely, the person who offended you doesn't even remember or care to remember the hurt and pain they have inflicted upon you. These people are probably moving on with their lives, living carefree, and searching for the next person to victimize. Do yourself a favor and forgive.

Forgiving the people who have caused you pain does not suggest that you are excusing their behavior or giving them a free pass for what they have done to you. When you forgive, it simply means you have decided to change your perspective and alter the

113

way you think about the situation. You have agreed to take control of your thoughts, attitudes, and actions which gives you back the power from the individuals who wounded you. Your emotions are no longer at the mercy of this offense. Please understand that once you have released the offender, you are not required to rebuild the relationship nor trust that person again. If you can reconcile and restore the relationship, that's great. If you can't, that's okay, too. God requires us to love and forgive, not trust.

TRUSTING OTHERS

After we have acknowledged the offense, accepted it, and decided to forgive, we now have the option to reconcile the relationship or just let it be and move on. Once you forgive someone, it doesn't mean you have to trust them again. Forgiveness and trust are two different concepts. I honestly believe people should have to earn your trust. You really understand how valuable trust is once someone has broken it. When people trust us, we shouldn't take it for granted because once that trust is violated, it's very difficult to restore. I'm not saying it's impossible to repair; however, it's going to be a process. After you are hurt or betrayed by someone, it's going to take some time to heal. The offender must understand this. We don't heal overnight, but if we allow God to help us, it won't take a lifetime. **Psalms 147:3** declares that God heals the brokenhearted and binds up their wounds and sorrows.

We now understand that God instructs us to forgive, and we must obey Him. Once we obey, our part is done, whether they respond or not. Remember, forgiveness is mostly for you and not others. It allows you to be free and to move forward in your life. Many people believe that once you forgive, things should go back to the way they were previously. This is not the case at all. If both parties decide they want to salvage the relationship and try to rebuild, then that's fine. But not all relationships have the potential to recover; therefore, you have to decide if restoring that relationship is worth your time and effort. Rebuilding that trust with someone will require some patience, tolerance, compassion, and mercy. Trust doesn't come easy. Forgiveness is a gift that you grant to a person, but your trust must be earned. One of the ways I know that I have truly forgiven someone is when I resist the urge to retaliate.

RESIST REVENGE

Forgiveness is when you no longer desire to punish the individuals for the hurt and pain, they have caused you. Ask yourself this question, "Do I wish to seek revenge or punish them for their wrongdoings?" If the answer is "yes," then you haven't truly "let it go." Once you lose the desire to punish and avenge your offenders, you have now begun the process of forgiveness and healing. The Bible warns us not to repay evil for evil, but instead, we should repay evil with good (**1 Peter 3:9**). Basically, "payback" doesn't pay. We lose when we decide to get back at someone for an offense. Don't lower yourself to their level and repay evil with evil because you will delay your blessings. It's not worth it. Don't miss your increase.

The Bible admonishes us to bless the people who hurt us and pray for them. It also instructs us to love our enemies and do good to the people that despitefully use us (**Matt. 5:44-45**). Now, I know this sounds ridiculous, but it actually works. Praying for our offenders allows us to release that burden and heavy load to God. We are basically communicating to Him that this burden is too heavy, and I need your help. When we pray for the people who wronged us, it lifts that weight and pressure off us that comes with holding a grudge. Our hearts are cleansed and renewed every time we pray for the people that have wounded us.

The more we pray, the more we begin to feel empathy and compassion toward them because prayer softens the heart. So, my advice to you is to pray for your offenders. Pray for their well-being and allow God to work on their hearts. You will eventually free yourself, and your life will be blessed. It's time to release that heavy load of unforgiveness.

Let's work to be at peace with one another. Once again, I'm not suggesting that you have to rebuild a relationship with someone who hurt you, but we must be peaceable. Seek reconciliation if possible; if not, just keep the peace. God commands us to do all that we can to live in harmony with everyone. Also, when our offenders are suffering, we must refuse to rejoice. This can be difficult because when the person who has hurt you is experiencing sorrow, there is a part of you that desires to see them suffer for the pain they've inflicted upon you. But when you refuse to rejoice in their sufferings, and instead pray for them, you will begin to see growth and increase in your life. Forgiveness is not a one- time event; sometimes you have to forgive over and over again, and that's okay. Be willing to do it as many times as it takes. Forgiveness is an act that must be continuously practiced in our everyday lives.

PRACTICE IT

Every day there is an opportunity for us to be offended by someone. This can happen at home, on your job, in the grocery store, or among friends; therefore, we have to keep a "let it go" attitude. Just let it roll off your shoulders, so to speak. Once the offense occurs, ask yourself, "Is staying angry worth my peace of mind?" "What will I benefit from holding this grudge?" Since there is no benefit in harboring anger, be willing to let it go. When you forgive, you are helping yourself. Forgiveness is something you do for your well-being. You stand to profit when you grant forgiveness to someone. You gain power, peace of mind, less stress, contentment, and freedom. Humble yourself and be ready to release mercy when the opportunity presents itself.

Forgiveness can be interchanged with the word mercy. I often think of forgiveness as an act of kindness, compassion, and tolerance extended toward the people who have offended you. We desire for others to show compassion toward us; therefore, we must be eager to reciprocate. One of my favorite verses in the Bible is to treat people how you would like to be treated (**Luke 6:31**). If you want mercy, give mercy. It's that simple. Yes, this principle can be challenging at times, but you can do it. Your life will be better for it. When forgiving others become a part of your lifestyle, there are many benefits attached.

BENEFITS

The more you forgive, the better you become at doing it. You begin to cultivate a heart of compassion, kindness, and tolerance every time you decide to let go of an offense. Forgiveness makes us happier. It's difficult to experience joy when harboring ill will toward others. Healthier relationships are developed when we practice forgiveness. Forgiveness sustains our friendships and allows us to have a better quality of life. We are friendlier people when we release offenses, and it causes others to enjoy our presence.

If you desire to experience less stress and anxiety in your life, decide right now that you're going to extend mercy to others, whether they deserve it or not. Extending mercy improves our overall health. Researchers say people that refuse to forgive will increase their risk of stress, depression, and insomnia. So, let's preserve our health and prevent these diseases by maintaining a forgiving heart. Overall, forgiveness allows us to grow and become the best version of ourselves.

Questions for Discussion & Reflection:

1. After reading this chapter, what insight did you gain as it relates to forgiving others?

2. What is forgiveness? And how do you know if you have truly forgiven someone?

3. Do you struggle with forgiveness? Please explain.

4. What are the benefits of forgiving others? How does unforgiveness negatively affect your life?

5. Who are the people that have hurt you in the past? What steps can you take to start the forgiveness process?

6. Have you forgiven yourself for the things you have done in the past? If not, how will you start that process?

7. Are you easily offended? Do you trust easily? What are some changes you need to make to improve in these areas?

CHAPTER 8

DEVELOPING QUALITY RELATIONSHIPS

According to Merriam-Webster, a relationship is a way in which two or more people, groups, or countries talk to, behave toward, connect, and deal with each other. It's an emotional, spiritual, or another type of connection between persons. Relationships can sometimes be difficult to maintain because we're all different people that are evolving daily. Majority of the issues and joys of life revolve around people and relationships. Our relationships have a significant effect on our quality of life; therefore, we should be selective and cautious about the individuals we allow to be a part of our inner circle. Yes, we do need relationships; there is no doubt about it. But we must use wisdom and be selective of who we choose to connect with.

RELATIONSHIP WITH GOD

Relationships influence our spiritual and personal development. This is why I believe a close relationship with God will help us to sustain all other relationships. For example, God is love, and when you have a relationship with Him, He will teach

121

you how to love others. God is peace; so, He will show you how to pursue peace with others. Your relationship with God is key when it comes to an understanding of how you should treat others. Seek God and get to know Him. Gain insight of His nature and His attributes so you can manifest His character in all of your associations. God is peace, love, compassionate, giving, merciful, and kind; therefore, the more time you spend with Him, the more you take on His nature. This is vital because when you possess these Christ-like qualities, it allows you to have more successful relationships.

Your relationship with God helps you to grow into a mature individual, and your growth determines how you interact with other people. Growth is essential. When you are developing as a person, you learn how to be more patient, kind, peaceful, and understanding. This is key to maintaining healthy and fulfilling relationships. One of the secrets to sustaining wholesome associations is being filled with God's love and expressing that love to others through your actions.

People will disappoint you, hurt you, and offend you; however, if you have God's love in your heart, you're better equipped to deal with these situations. Strive to love others the way that God loves you. He loves us with unconditional love. Now, I know this can be challenging at times, but it's worth the effort.

Your relationships will be better for it. I've come to understand that when your love is unconditional, you're able to forgive the faults of others much easier. And remember, it's not about feelings, it's about our actions. Love is an action. It's not just something you say; it's something you do. The Bible teaches us in **1 Corinthians 13:4-8**:

> *"Love suffers long and is kind; love does not envy; love does not parade itself, is not puffed up; does not behave rudely, does not seek its own, it not provoked, thinks no evil; does not rejoice in iniquity, but rejoices in the truth; bears all things, believes all things, hopes all things, endures all things... Love never fails..."*

As you can see, God's kind of love is unselfish. It cares about the feelings of others in spite of their actions. We must remember that we're all flawed, imperfect, and blemished in one way or another. This is why unconditional love is necessary. The closer we get to God, the more Christ-like we become; And as a result, we're able to maintain better relationships. I've discovered that our dealings with other people are a direct reflection of our relationship with God.

For example, if you're a selfish person, and your relationships are all about you, this tells me that you only seek God for what He can do for you. You're not concerned about how you can help others and advance the Kingdom of God. Okay, let's take a look at another example. Let's say you're a person that believes you're always right and never wrong in your dealings with others. You come across as a know it all, you don't have a teachable spirit, and you always have all the right answers— so you think. This is a humility issue, and this kind of behavior implies that your relationships are only about you. It also suggests that your relationship with God is all about you. It seems that you only seek God when you've exhausted all of your other possibilities, instead of initially seeking and depending on Him for leadership and guidance in everything you do.

Watch out for individuals who believe they're never wrong, and believe they can do no wrong. Stay away from people who seem to think they have all the answers to life's problems. Run as fast as you can. Avoid them. Try your best to steer clear of these types of relationships. People with a know-it-all mentality tend to be prideful, and their prideful attitude will undoubtedly spill over into other relationships. A prideful person relies on their own knowledge and understanding when responding to life's issues. Seeking God for answers is their last resort. I'm a firm believer that you must trust that God has all the answers; and not you.

Please don't misunderstand me. I'm not implying that we shouldn't have knowledge or understanding about certain issues that arise. No, I'm saying that we must be willing to set our opinions aside and seek the wisdom of God. Also, we need to consider the opinions of others, and stop thinking we have the right answers all the time. Learn to seek the wisdom of God before you assume to know what's best for you and someone else. As for me, I trust God to know what's best for me; and I'm confident that He will reveal to me the answers that I am seeking. God will always guide us in the right direction; guaranteed. You just have to trust Him. In **Proverbs 3:5-6**, the author encourages us to *"Trust in the Lord with all thine heart; and lean not unto thine own understanding. In all thy ways acknowledge him, and he shall direct thy paths."*

LOVE FOR OTHERS

Your relationship with God is instrumental in how you manage your other relationships. When we're close to God, He teaches us how to be humble, patient, and forgiving. All of these qualities are essential when interacting with others. We must have the right attitude, or our relationships will suffer. Allow God's character to grow in you, and make an effort to love others the way God loves you. Once we receive and accept God's love, we're able to spread that love to others; but if you're having a difficult time receiving God's love, you'll have a difficult sharing His love.

For example, if it's hard for you to believe that God forgives you despite your flaws and past mistakes, you'll find it very challenging to forgive others of their faults. You must be able to receive God's forgiveness, so you can extend that same love and mercy to the people that are in your life. Remember, a heart that's filled with God's love will always love others with that same love.

When we love one another, it's an indication that we know God because God is love. Please don't say you are close to God, yet you hate other people. This is not consistent with the principles of God. The Bible says, *"If someone says, "I love God," and hates his brother, he is a liar; for the one who does not love his brother whom he has seen, cannot love God whom he has not seen"* (**1 John 4:20**) I totally agree with this truth. We are incredibly deceived if we believe that we can hate our family, colleagues, and friends, but say we are filled with God's love. This is not possible. It's deception. The same love you have for God— whom you've never seen—should transfer to the people you connect with regularly.

Learn how to be patient with people. We should all strive to make allowances for each other faults. Remember, we are imperfect people trying to do the very best we can with the information we have. No one is without error. As long as we're here on earth, we are sure to disappoint and hurt each other at some point. Sometimes intentionally, sometimes unintentionally, but it will happen. We must develop patience if we desire to maintain healthy relationships.

Let me ask you this question: why is it that we desire for others to be patient and longsuffering with us, but we don't want to reciprocate? It goes back to the golden rule: treat others like you would like to be treated. If we could just keep this principle in mind, our relationships would be so much better. Regardless of what people do, our aim should always be to treat them like we want to be treated, and not like they treat us. For instance, if a person disrespects you and you decide to disrespect them back, then you are no better than them. Now, you have stooped to their level. You've allowed their character to influence your behavior. Remember, we all must reap what we sow. You are accountable for what you do, not what they do. Just make sure you make the right decisions, whether they choose to or not. Relationships require effort, so be willing to put in the work.

BUILDING GOOD FRIENDSHIPS

If you want to build solid relationships, it will demand time and energy from all parties involved, but it's worth the work. Spend time with one another. How do you truly know someone if you never spend time with them? I know that we're all leading busy lives with so much to do; however, if we plan on sustaining quality relationships, we must make time for each other. There's no way around it.

In order to truly know the people that you're in a relationship with, there must be open communication. Both parties must be willing to share personal things about their lives. Relationships require intimacy. And I'm not talking about physical intimacy. I'm talking about closeness, sharing intimate details about your life experiences with one another. We need to ask questions and be willing to give honest answers. If you genuinely want authentic relationships, then you must be real. I urge you to be yourself and don't be afraid to express your true feelings about various subject matters. Let them see who you really are!

Be willing to rejoice with your friends. Make sure you complement each other on your victories and accomplishments. And also encourage each other during the difficult seasons. You will have happy moments and sad moments, laughter and crying, ups and downs. This is what friendship is all about. No relationship is happy and joyful all the time; therefore, you should anticipate seasons of mourning and sadness. In **Romans 12:15**, the writer urges, *"Rejoice with them that do rejoice, and weep with them that weep."*

Seasons change and people change. Life happens. When we truly understand this, we're more inclined to stand with each other through difficult times because it's just a season. During the challenging seasons of our relationships, we will experience frustration and pain. Pain is a part of relationships. It comes with the territory, but we should always grow from the pain. I call it "growing pains." Never leave the situation the same. Learn the lessons and extract the wisdom from those painful moments. Remember, challenging times are only temporary. They come and go. Enjoy the journey and continue to grow through each phase of your relationships.

Cover each other's faults. If your friends hurt you, refuse to gossip and share this information with outsiders, unless they are attempting to counsel you. The Bible tells us that *"love covers a multitude of sins"* (**1 Pet. 4:8**). This means that your love for that person should conceal their wrongdoings and transgressions toward you. Let's be honest, you wouldn't want your friends to go behind your back and gossip about your faults. Well, of course not! Therefore, if they offend you, confront them or pray to God about the matter. Allow Him to guide you on what steps to take. Gossiping about the offense only makes matters worse. When you go to other people about your relationship issues, it can result in people spreading discord or expressing wrong opinions about someone they do not know. This will, inevitably, create more contention and confusion.

129

When we seek out the opinion of others about our relationship problems, the response is usually partial. They only hear one side of the story, and we know there are three versions to every story. There is your version, their version, and the truth. The person that's hearing your version is listening to the issue from your angle. That's why I advise you to discuss your concerns with the person you have the problem with and make an attempt to resolve the matter yourselves. Try to understand why your friends act the way they do. This is vital. It will cause you to be more empathetic towards them.

There is usually a reason as to why people do what they do. I'm not justifying the actions of the people who wronged you, but I am suggesting that you consider the reason for their actions. Often, we focus more on what the person has done, rather than the reason it was done in the first place. When you seek to understand why people do what they do, you become more patient, tolerant, caring, and understanding. These are all Christ-like qualities that we should desire to cultivate in our lives.

It is beneficial to seek wisdom and understanding in all of our personal and social matters. Especially if the relationship is important to you. **Proverbs 4:7** says, *"Wisdom is the principal thing; therefore, get wisdom: and with all thy getting get understanding."* Wisdom is vital. It's challenging to develop healthy friendships when you fail to gain an understanding of one another. Learn to appreciate and accept each other, regardless of your differences.

ACCEPTANCE

Accept people for who they are, and strive to celebrate your differences. This is very challenging because we're all unique, and we tend to befriend people who are the same as us. It's more comfortable for us to bond with like-minded people rather than take the time and effort to understand people with diverse backgrounds and beliefs. We need to step out of our comfort zones and become acquainted with people who perceive the world differently than we do. This is something that I've started to incorporate in my own life.

Yes, we're all different; but that's what makes us special. Make an effort to befriend someone who doesn't always see your point of view. Disagreeing with each other is okay. Just agree to disagree. These situations allow you to think outside the box and see things from another person's perspective. Wouldn't life be boring if everyone were alike? How could we learn from one another if our views were all identical? Diversity is good. Make every attempt to accept and appreciate other peoples' differences. I challenge you to welcome diversity into your life.

Treat others with respect, and seek to add value to their lives. This all starts with you. If you have respect for yourself, then you'll have no problem with respecting others; and if you value yourself, you'll have no problem with adding value to others. We're all made in God's image; therefore, we should always strive to honor one another. It doesn't cost you anything to value people. Honestly, I don't want to be in a relationship with anyone that doesn't respect me. I'm valuable, and my goal is to add value to people every chance I get. A relationship that lacks mutual respect will eventually disintegrate and die.

A person who recognizes their significance will not allow or tolerate another person to disrespect them. They know their worth, and they have no problem with discontinuing that relationship. However, some people allow other individuals to degrade and dishonor them. These are individuals that struggle with low self-worth. They believe that any attention is better than no attention, even if it's negative. This is not the right mindset to have. People tend to treat you the way you allow them to treat you. I suggest you teach others how to handle you. Value yourself!

We must learn to respect others, regardless of who they are. And stop trying to change people into who we think they should be. Once again, we're all uniquely made. Let's accept people, and celebrate their uniqueness. When you have a clear understanding of your identity, you're able to appreciate people for who they are. People who value others are usually confident in their identity, and they tend to acknowledge, celebrate, and hold high regard for others. They don't need constant validation and affirmation about who they are because they already know. These are confident individuals!

Associate yourself with confident people, and work on cultivating confidence in your own life. Try to avoid people who attempt to change you because they don't want to accept you for who you are. Their goal is to control you; this is a form of manipulation. There are some relationships where one person controls the actions of the other person. They don't allow them to be themselves, which creates a very unhealthy and co-dependent relationship.

A co-dependent relationship is when one person is relying on the other person for identity and validation. One of the individuals usually have low self-esteem, so they depend on the controlling person to validate them and make them feel better about who they are. This type of bond brings a level of fear, intimidation, and control to the relationship. The other party usually controls the person that's always seeking validation and approval. The weaker person is terrified of confronting their friend about any issues because they fear to lose the friendship. They have become needy. People that desire to control you don't have any control over themselves, and that's why they seek to control you. Avoid these kinds of people. And if you find yourself in this type of relationship, discontinue it immediately.

A relationship where one person enables another person's irresponsible and negligent behavior is a sign of a co-dependent relationship. For example, let's say you have a friend who constantly borrows money from you and never pays you back. The money they borrow from you is being used to support their terrible addictions that you are aware of. This individual continually makes excuses as to why they can't pay you back and continues to borrow money from you. When you continue to lend them money, despite their lack of effort to pay you back, you are supporting and enabling their wrongful behavior. You are basically saying that it's okay for them to be addicted, borrow money, and never pay back. Now, I question if you really care for this person as your friend because you are ultimately helping them to destroy their life. If your friend is behaving in a way that's upsetting to you, be willing to confront them, and communicate your concerns in a respectful manner. They need to know that their immoral behavior is unacceptable.

COMMUNICATE MORE EFFECTIVELY

Every relationship needs to have open and honest communication. Communication involves speaking and listening to one another. Make a concerted effort to understand each other. This usually requires more listening than speaking. Listening is a skill that must be developed if we desire to maintain quality relationships. If you're always talking, then how can you hear the other persons' concerns. People appreciate individuals who listen to them. It's a sign that they care. I believe that we were born with two ears and one mouth for a reason. I think God intentionally created us this way so we could listen twice as much as we speak. Become a great listener.

Poor communication can cause you to make assumptions about what the other person intended to say. We are not mind-readers. If you're not comprehending what the other person is trying to convey, vocalize your need to understand. Always listen and seek to understand one another. This is vital when it comes to developing successful relationships. When you intently listen to others, it implies that you care about the things that concern them. It makes the other person feel important and valued by you.

Give feedback to each other. Good or bad. This encourages growth and allows you to help each other to achieve your highest potential. When you take the time to give feedback to a friend, whether it's positive or constructive criticism, it shows that you care about the concerns of your friend, and you want to help them come up with the best possible solutions. For the most part, friends can appreciate when you're honest with them. Just make sure you point out the positive things first before you give the constructive criticism.

If you're the person on the receiving end, refuse to be confrontational about the feedback that is given to you. It's your decision on whether or not you choose to utilize the input provided. You must consider that they are trying to help you the best way they know how. I always like to say, "Eat the meat and throw away the bones." Basically, this means you take what you need and don't worry about the rest. Discard the information you don't need. This kind of mindset keeps your relationships secure and peaceful.

SAFE RELATIONSHIPS

Choose to be in relationships with people who are safe. Safe people are individuals that draw us closer to God and inspire us to be the best version of ourselves. They add value to our lives. When you are associated with people who are unsafe, it will drain you mentally, spiritually, and emotionally. Some people are not beneficial for us, and we need to recognize them when they appear.

If the people you associate with are not helping you, they are hurting you. Unsafe people will not influence you to draw closer to God. They are usually moving you in the opposite direction— away from God. This is not good.

Unsafe people tend to have a negative influence on your life. Refuse to associate with these types of individuals. Learn to recognize unsafe people and avoid building relationships with them. The Bible admonishes us not to keep company with immoral people because their character will eventually influence our behavior. *Bad company corrupts good character (*1

Corinthians 15:33). The people that you decide to spend the majority of your time with will ultimately determine your success in life because they influence your life. That's why it's imperative that we surround ourselves with individuals who desire to reach their full potential. Associate with people that's pursuing their purpose in life. Bond with individuals that want more out of life. These are the people you need to connect with.

Decide to connect with people who will influence you to become the best version of yourself. Build relationships with individuals who are kind, empathetic, caring, forgiving, patient, and motivated. These are the qualities that all of us should be cultivating in our lives. If the people you affiliate with have a positive influence on your life, then you're on the right track. Growth is inevitable.

Questions for Discussion & Reflection:

1. After reading this chapter, what insight did you gain as it relates to developing and maintaining the right relationships?

2. How does your relationship with God affect your relationship with other people? Explain.

3. Do you value your relationships? How can your relationships become better?

4. Do you pursue diverse relationships? How can you benefit from diverse relationships?

5. Do you accept people for who they are? Or, do you try to change them?

6. What is a co-dependent relationship? Are you currently involved in one? If so, what steps do you plan to take to improve this relationship?

7. Are there some relationships that you need to discontinue? Why?

CHAPTER 9

IDENTIFYING DISTRACTIONS

The Cambridge English Dictionary defines distraction as something that prevents you from giving full attention to something else. Distractions will pull you in a different direction and take you off course. They can become dangerous to your destiny. Don't allow distractions to interrupt your progress and take your focus away from what's truly important. There will always be situations to arise in your life to distract you from what you need to be concentrating on at that moment. Stay focused. Distractions appear in many different forms, such as family, friends, colleagues, entertainment, comparisons, and more. We must always be aware of the countless interruptions that come to alter our course and delay our purpose in life.

PURPOSE OF DISTRACTIONS

What is the purpose of a distraction? The purpose of a distraction is to divert you from fulfilling your purpose in life. That's why you must pay attention to your life and remain vigilant so you'll be able to discern distractions when they appear. God has a purpose for your life, and if you're not careful, you will allow people and things to hinder you from fulfilling that purpose. Recognize the distractions that enter your life and deal with them accordingly. If you continue to lose focus and cater to these disruptions, they will rob you of your destiny. This is a serious matter.

If you are a person with goals, dreams, and aspirations, then you most definitely need to stay alert at all times. Distractions are always lurking, seeking an opportunity to impede your progress. When we're moving forward in the plan of God for our lives, many opposing forces will surface in hopes of hindering us from reaching our goals. Focus is the key. We must be disciplined and focused if we're going to have a chance at defeating distractions. The goal is to eliminate as many distractions as possible. Now, you will have a difficult time trying to remove all distractions, but you can eliminate most of them if you're attentive. Stay alert, and don't fret about the small stuff.

Focusing your attention on trivial matters can be a distraction. For example, let's say you're in the middle of writing a paper that's due in several days, and you begin to ponder about how your friend offended you several months ago—that's a distraction. You and the friend have already resolved the matter, and supposedly moved on; however, you're still meditating on that offense. Your mind should be on the assignment before you. If you're not careful, you will continue to think on that offense and evoke emotions that will hinder you from focusing on the task at hand. And before you know it, you have wasted countless hours recapping that offense in your mind that happened months ago. This has cost you time and energy that should have been used to complete your assignment.

When a distraction steals your time, it has accomplished its goal. Time is valuable, and once it's gone, it's gone. You don't get it back. Don't allow this to happen to you. Stay on track. Resist the temptation to offer attention to people and situations who don't matter in the grand scheme of things. Some people show up just to distract you. They appear simply to waste your time. Discern them, and choose your battles wisely. Only engage and involve yourself in situations that directly affect your productivity, family, and purpose in life.

For instance, if you're having car issues that are presently stressing you out because you need transportation for the kids and your job, then you must stop and take the time to ponder ways to correct this issue. If you don't resolve this matter, it will distract you from giving full attention to whatever you are supposed to be working on at that time. This transportation issue is directly affecting your family and productivity; therefore, it should be resolved promptly. This is not a trivial matter; you won't be able to concentrate on other projects until this problem is settled. If you can conquer the distractions in your mind, you can conquer them in your life. The battle is won in your mind first.

STARTS IN YOUR MIND

I've discovered over the years that some of the thoughts we choose to meditate on can be some of our greatest distractions. Pay attention to your thought life. Do not allow your thinking to interfere with your current assignments. When you notice yourself meditating on the wrong thoughts, that's when you need to cast away those ideas and refocus your attention. Also, stop wasting time pondering things you have no control over. This is another distraction.

Worrying about other people's destructive behavior will not help you or change them. You only have control over your actions; therefore, concern yourself with the things that you have the power to change. If a person's actions are causing disturbances in your life, you might consider separating yourself from that individual or group of individuals. You have control over this matter. Sometimes you just have to walk away. It's not personal; it's business. Your destiny is on the line. Every person has the right to determine who enters and remains in their life.

In order for you to prevent your meditations from becoming a distraction, regularly monitor your thoughts. The well-known Christian speaker and author Joyce Meyers states,

"Think about what you're thinking about." Choose your thoughts carefully, and refuse to allow negative thoughts to run rampant in your mind. Attempt to think positive. **Philippians 4:8** advises, *"Finally, brethren, whatsoever things are true, whatsoever things are honest, whatsoever things are just, whatsoever things are pure, whatsoever things are lovely, whatsoever things are of good report; if there be any virtue, and if there be any praise, think on these things."*

Wrong thinking will directly affect the way you feel. When you are experiencing unpleasant feelings, it's time to consult your thoughts. The people or situations that you are mulling over at that moment are producing unwanted feelings. You have control over this. When you change your thoughts, your feelings will change. We have more control over what happens in our life than we realize. Our mind is subject to us. We don't have to allow stinking thinking to affect our lives adversely. If it's not beneficial, don't meditate on it. Cast down those thoughts. Again, it all starts in your mind.

If you want to change your actions, you have to change the way you think about certain situations. Why is this important? Your thinking affects your feelings, and your feelings can trigger certain behaviors. Majority of people tend to act on their feelings. And this will always get you into trouble. Feelings are fickle, and they can't be trusted. Your feelings will cause you to say and do things that you will later regret. That's why it's so important to monitor your thoughts.

If you're feeling angry or disappointed, then it's tough for you to show kindness toward others, especially if you are a person whose actions are motivated by feelings. For instance, let's say you have been praying to God to send someone your way that needs help. So, God finally sends a person down your path that needs encouragement, but you missed your opportunity to be a blessing to that individual. You know why? You were distracted by your thoughts, and consumed with negative feelings. This caused you to miss your opportunity to help someone

Sometimes when we look too far into the future, it can become a major distraction. We tend to worry about tomorrow before tomorrow even arrives. I'm not suggesting that we don't plan, but I am suggesting that we focus on the day at hand. Worrying about tomorrow is a total distraction. When you fret about what might happen in the near future, you are fighting battles before they begin. Once again, you are tormenting yourself about something that you have no control over. Do your best to prepare for unforeseen circumstances, but live in the present moment.

Remember, worrying doesn't solve anything. It only keeps your mind preoccupied with the wrong thoughts. And this distracts you from focusing on the things that need your attention right now. In **Matthew 6:31-34**, Jesus cautions,

"Therefore, do not worry, saying, 'What shall we eat?' or 'What shall we drink' or 'What shall we wear?' For after all these things the Gentiles seek. For your heavenly Father knows that you need all these things. But seek first the kingdom of God and His righteousness, and all these things shall be added to you. Therefore, do not worry about tomorrow, for tomorrow will worry about its own things. Sufficient for the day is its own trouble."

In other words, we should be concerned about tomorrow when it arrives and not a minute sooner. Again, I'm not advising you not to make plans for your life because I certainly have plans. I'm simply suggesting that you refuse to allow the future to stress you out and rob you of your present happiness. Stop looking so far ahead, and trust that God has a good plan for your life. Make plans, but allow God to change your plans if necessary. And remember, whatever obstacles come our way, God will help us to overcome it.

Our job is to seek God and make sure our actions line up with His principles. Everything else will work itself out. Nothing good comes from worrying. It's a waste of time and energy, and it stagnates your life. No one ever makes progress by worrying. So, stop doing it. Remember, God is Sovereign, and He can do as He pleases. God already knows everything we need before we ask.

When we acknowledge this truth, we will begin to experience more joy and peace in our lives.

FIGHTING DISTRACTIONS

We must learn how to effectively and strategically fight against distractions. The people and situations that are currently interfering with your purpose and peace of mind must go. It's not worth it. Any position or relationship that fails to develop you as a person is harmful to your destiny. Limiting your contact with certain individuals who are hindering your progress will be one way to fight against distractions. For instance, several years ago, I had a friend who continuously found fault in me. She rarely encouraged me and seldom rejoiced when God blessed my life. Her conversations were mostly negative and self-righteous, which always caused me to feel down and depressed when I left her presence. When I would confront her about the matter, she would often say, "That's just my personality." To me, that's just an excuse to remain the way you are. We all have control over our words and actions. This situation is a prime example of needing to "let go" of a relationship that is disturbing your peace and joy. We need people that are releasing positive vibes in our life.

If you are working for a business that causes you a lot of stress and anxiety, it can be a significant distraction in your life. And it will eventually affect your peace of mind. One way to fight against this undue tension would be to consider changing jobs. If you're always stressing, hating to go to work every day, then you're not living a productive life. You're just existing. No one can fulfill their purpose in life if they are just existing and surviving from day to day. Finding a job that allows you to have peace of mind would be more suitable; even if it pays a lower salary. Now, I'm not telling you to avoid challenges in life, but there is a difference between overcoming challenges at a job versus you subjecting yourself to a hectic environment that's affecting your overall quality of life.

When you have a vision for your life, you have to be extra careful on what environments you operate in. Vision requires creativity, and excessive stress can diminish your creativity. Remember, you have to think long term. It would be worth your future to say goodbye to stressful situations that can potentially destroy your plans and goals. Remaining in a hostile environment is detrimental to your destiny; it's a waste of time and energy. Recognize these distractions.

How are you expending your time? Please be mindful of the time you spend on certain people and situations. Some individuals enter our lives just to waste our time. And when we continue to allow people to do this, it distracts us from pursuing our dreams. Be aware of time stealers and dream killers. People that don't have a vision for their lives have no problem with distracting you from your dream. Avoid these types of relationships. Spend your days with people who are moving in the same direction as you. Seek relationships that are beneficial for you and the other person as well. We only get one life, so we must use our time wisely. This doesn't mean we shouldn't make time for people, but we must be selective on who we share our time with. Your time is precious, and once it's gone, you can't get it back.

If you have friends that are always trying to influence you to party and have fun, but never work on goals and dreams, then you may need to rethink those relationships. It's may be time to let them go or limit your contact with these individuals. Now, there's nothing wrong with having fun, but everything should be done in moderation. There's a time and place for everything. If we're always having fun, then how can we pursue our destiny. To make progress, you may need to terminate some friendships. Yes, it will be difficult, but you must consider what's more important. Think about it, if your friends have all this free time to party and have fun, that means they're not pursuing their goals. Their purpose is not a priority for them; however, this should definitely be a problem for you. It's time to reevaluate some of your relationships and get your priorities in line.

Are you involved with people who are adding to your life or subtracting from your life? This is a vital question. If you are among people who take more away from you than they give, it will leave you exhausted. Relationships should be balanced. Both of you must add something to each other's lives; otherwise, one person will start to experience feelings of resentment and abuse. When you remain silent and harbor these feelings of anger, it prevents you from focusing on what's more important in that season.

One-sided relationships are not healthy, and they can be a distraction in your life. If there is a person in your life that always take, but never give back, then you must be willing to confront this friend. Otherwise, their actions will ultimately destroy the relationship. Once you address the matter, observe to see if their behavior changes. If it doesn't, I suggest that you severe the relationship. No person, place, or thing is more important than your destiny and your relationship with God. If you are not sure what to do in any given situation, pray to God for wisdom; He will grant it to you. **James 1:5** teaches, "*If any of you lack wisdom, let him ask of God, that giveth to all men liberally, and upbraideth not; and it shall be given him.*" Ask, and He will give!

WISDOM

We must use wisdom when it comes to protecting our future from distractions. Distractions are not always obvious. For instance, let's say you decide to be a teacher, but God called you to be a doctor. Teaching is a good thing, but it's not the best thing for your life. You're called to be a doctor. Working on something good is not acceptable if you're called to do something great. Therefore, if you're spending your time preparing to be a teacher, you are distracted from your real purpose. Being a teacher is not what God called you to be. Remember, He has a plan for your life. And if you stick to His plan, you will be fulfilled, satisfied, prosperous, and content.

I now realize that "good" is the enemy of "great." You could be involved in an activity that's good, but it may not be conducive to your purpose in life. Remember, we don't want to do a "good thing;" we want to do the "best thing" for our lives. Make sure you work on projects that will help you to fulfill the vision for your life. Everything you involve yourself with should line up with your destiny; otherwise, you are wasting your time.

I'm reminded of a quote written by Thomas Merton, an American Catholic writer, and theologian, that states, "People may spend their whole lives climbing the ladder of success only to find—once they reach the top—that the ladder is leaning against the wrong wall." What a true statement. It would be a tragedy to come to the end of your life and realize that you have been working on the wrong assignments, associating with the wrong people, pursuing the wrong career, and serving the wrong God. Don't allow this to happen to you.

Let me pose a few questions: what are you working on at the present moment? Are you pursuing goals that will move you toward your destiny? Or are you seeking things that are distracting you from your true purpose in life? Make certain that the people and activities that you are presently involved with are not preventing you from doing what's best for you in this season.

There is a verse in the Bible that reads, *"All things are lawful for me, but all things are not expedient: all things are lawful for me, but all things edify not"* (**1 Corinthians 10:23**). In other words, the task you're working on may not be wrong, it may not be a sin, and it may not be unlawful; but is it beneficial and conducive to what God has purposed you to do in this season? Keep in mind, just because it's a good thing doesn't mean it's the best thing for you. Please don't get distracted by doing something good when you could be working on something great. Be aware of distractions!

COMMON DISTRACTIONS

Once again, we're going to be challenged with many distractions along our journey; but our job is to identify these distractions and avoid them. One common distraction in life is our pursuit of money and riches. If we're not careful, we will attempt the wrong endeavors just to gain wealth. Wealth is not bad as long as you don't become a slave to it. When your pursuit of money becomes an obsession, you will choose vocations based on money rather than purpose. You will start involving yourself in projects and jobs solely for monetary gain. This is a distraction from your true calling in life.

The temptation of wealth has caused many people to forfeit their destiny just to gain a dollar. People who chase money over purpose are choosing to serve money instead of God. You can't serve both. The writer in **Luke 16:13** contends, *"No servant can serve two masters: for either he will hate the one, and love the other; or else he will hold to the one, and despise the other. Ye cannot serve God and mammon."* In this text, "mammon" refers to money or worldly riches. Your primary focus should be God's purpose for your life and not money. If you pursue purpose, money will chase you; you'll never have to chase it.

Another common distraction would be focusing on the cares of this world. Some of us are consumed with the happenings of the world, like keeping up with the "Joneses" or our next-door neighbors. Comparing yourself to others is a distraction, and you shouldn't do it. Keeping track of who has the larger houses, cars, businesses, gifts, and talents will cause you to be in unwanted predicaments that are not beneficial for you and your family. Focus on your own life. Stop getting in debt to prove something to people that don't care anything about you.

For example, you've made a plan to save money to finance your dreams. One day you noticed that your neighbor has just purchased a new car, and now you decide to buy a new vehicle just because they have one. This is a competitive attitude, and this kind of behavior will cause you to accumulate unwanted debt. Your goal was to save money to finance your dreams, but since you have a competitive nature and a craving to be the best, you have pushed your dreams to the back burner. What a tragedy. Your attention should be on your purpose and not your neighbor's new vehicle. This distraction has caused you to sacrifice your current goals to save money. This is not acceptable, especially if you desire to accomplish your dreams in life. Your purpose should be your priority.

If you're not careful, your desire for achievements and possessions can become a distraction in your life. It's okay to accomplish things and achieve goals, but we must make sure it doesn't cause us to possess a prideful and arrogant attitude. If you're not accomplishing goals to move you closer to destiny, then you are susceptible to pride and self-centeredness. Your achievements must be purpose driven; otherwise, you will get captivated by the accolades and praises from other people. This can cause you to become self-consumed, and then you'll begin to elevate yourself above others. Just remember, all the compliments and tributes you receive from your successes will only produce temporary happiness, that's why your motivation has to come from a deeper place.

When a higher purpose inspires your achievements, you'll always be fulfilled even after the praises and accolades disappear. Once you seek God and do the work that He has called you to do, you will begin to experience true joy and contentment. We won't experience this joy if we pursue accomplishments devoid of purpose. Watch out for discontentment. It will cause you to pursue the wrong things in life, which can result in you delaying your destiny.

Be content in the season that God has you in, and recognize that you're progressing toward greater things. When your attention is on God, He will lead you in the right direction and give you what you need to fulfill your assignment. Our job is to seek the Kingdom of God first and live righteously, then everything we need will be added to our lives in the proper season (**Matthew 6:33**). Make God your priority, and everything else will fall into place.

154

We'll always contend with distractions throughout our journey. They will continuously show up, but we must identify them and choose not to expend time and energy on these distractions. Remember, these interruptions only come to pull your attention away from what you truly need to be focused on. If you are a person that's single-minded, dedicated, and focused, you will reap many benefits in your life.

BENEFITS OF BEING FOCUSED

Maintaining your focus will allow you to achieve your goals on time. More opportunities will open up for you when you're committed and purpose driven. Your confidence increases when you are focused because you feel like you have control over your life. You are getting things done; your life is progressing. Remain persistent. It helps you to complete tasks and not become distracted by the daily challenges that life brings. People who are devoted and driven know how to manage their time wisely, and they finish what they've started. If you continue to be dedicated and centered, you will experience better relationships, internal growth, and a sense of hope in your life. Stay focused!

Questions for Discussion & Reflection:

1. After reading this chapter, what insight did you gain as it relates to identifying distractions in your life?

2. How can you avoid distractions? What are some ways you can fight against them?

3. Distractions come in many forms. How have they shown up in your life? Identify them.

4. What steps will you take to refocus your attention in this season?

5. How can worrying become a distraction in your life?

6. Have you been distracted by the pursuit of riches? Do you compete and compare your life to others? If so, how has it been a distraction for you?

7. How have distractions adversely affected your life in the past and present?

8. What are the benefits of remaining focused?

CHAPTER 10

DEVELOPING THE SPIRIT OF EXCELLENCE

Are you a person of excellence? Do you strive to be better? A person of excellence is determined to do the very best they can with what they have. So, let's define excellence? Excellence is when you exceed the requirements and go above the call of duty. Majority of people only do what's expected of them, but a person of excellence goes the extra mile. They always give one hundred percent or more. When you have an excellent mindset, it compels you to do your very best in everything you set out to accomplish. Strive to be exceptional in every area of your life including your job, in school, at home, at church, and in your relationships. If you excel in your everyday tasks— regardless if someone's watching or not— you're operating in excellence.

Excellence is cultivated in the heart first and subsequently revealed through your actions. It's not enough to just produce good work; attempt to produce great work. To do this, you must nurture a spirit of excellence. A spirit of excellence simply means you're not satisfied with mediocre performance. You require the very best from yourself and the people around you; you refuse to be average and accept average.

Maintaining a spirit of excellence allows you to grow and develop in character. It becomes a part of who you are and what you stand for. A person of excellence is a valuable individual, and they never have to worry about finding work or being employed because they are seen as an asset to the organization. When you make yourself a person of value, others will be inspired, and more opportunities will be presented to you. Remain committed to the process of developing yourself, and you'll become an exceptional individual.

COMMITMENT

There are certain characteristics that a person of excellence must possess. One of them is commitment. If you say you're going to do something, then do it. Keep your word. This communicates to others that you're a person that can be trusted. And they can depend on you. Being committed means, you will follow through on your promises regardless of how you feel about it later. I remember reading this anonymous quote that stated, "Commitment means staying loyal to what you said you were going to do long after the mood you said it in has left you." What a true statement. We don't act on how we feel; we act on what we know to be true. And the truth about commitment is that people respect you when you keep your promises. They see you as a person of integrity.

People who make good on their commitments are usually loyal to themselves first. When you fail to follow through on your obligations to others, you're not only disappointing that person, but you're disappointing yourself as well. Commitment begins with you. Devotion to God and yourself usually results in you being devoted to others. Just remember that the most vital commitment of our lives is our faithfulness to God and His principles. The Bible declares, "*You shall walk after the Lord your God, and fear him, and keep his commandments, and obey his voice, and ye shall serve him, and cleave unto him*" (**Deuteronomy 13:4**). I've experienced in my own life that when you remain loyal to God and adhere to His principles, you'll begin to see this same attitude surface in other areas of your life.

THE RIGHT THING

Doing the right thing when it's not popular is difficult, but we must do it regardless of what people might say. An upright individual is not easily swayed by the opinion of others, and they strive to do what's right no matter what. They are determined to walk in truth, in spite of criticism. For example, let's say you go to the store and purchase a couple of shirts. On your way to the car, you realize that the clerk failed to charge you for one of the shirts.

What do you do? Do you listen to your friend who claims it was a blessing and advise you to keep the shirt and not return it? Or do you go back to the store, explain the situation to the clerk, and pay for that item? If you're walking in integrity, you would return the shirt or purchase it; otherwise, it would be considered theft. Do the right thing!

Taking a product that you didn't pay for is stealing unless it was given to you as a gift. This is true regardless of how you may try to justify it. Responding correctly to these types of situations over time develops your character and transforms you into a person of excellence. When this happens, people will begin to perceive you as a trustworthy person. And remember, saying the right thing and doing the right thing is not the same. It's easy to communicate thoughts that we never act out. My friend would always say, "It's easier said than done." I agree. Make sure your words are in agreement with your actions; otherwise, your words carry no weight.

DEPENDABLE

Are you dependable? Can others rely on you to do what you said you were going to do? Reliable individuals usually keep their word. They are responsible individuals that you can depend on. Dependability is a quality that we all must cultivate in our lives if we desire to become a person of excellence. A person that's trustworthy will always keep their word; their nature reflects the nature of God. God always makes good on His promises. Yes, I know that we're not perfect like God, but there is nothing wrong with striving for perfection. Our goal is to become like Christ. We should embody the attributes of Christ.

Pursue relationships with people whom you can trust and depend on in difficult times. You can't determine if a person is dependable when things are going well. Trouble-free seasons rarely show you a person's true character. Anybody can be great when things are going well, but it's when the challenges arise, that we often discover a person's real nature. Are your friends dependable during the tough seasons of life? Our actions often reflect who we are during trying times.

LEAD BY EXAMPLE

Are you a leader or a follower? How do you know if you're a leader? Pay attention to your actions. A great leader is a front-runner that leads by example. They don't just communicate the truth; they live by the truth. Leaders should be a model for others to follow. They must refuse to settle for good enough. Great leaders have high standards and will not compromise on their convictions for anyone. They're always conscious of what they speak and how they treat others. They accept responsibility because they hold themselves accountable to God first. How can you identify whether or not a person is a good leader? Observe their lifestyle. You will know them by their fruit, which is their conduct (**Matt. 7:16**). Ask yourself, do they follow the principles they teach?

What type of fruit are you displaying to others? Does your fruit support the words you speak? I always like to say, "Don't just talk the talk, but walk the walk." Make sure you practice what you teach. Often people say the right things, but struggle to demonstrate what they claim to believe. Sometimes it's just better to let our walking do the talking. Stop trying to convince people of who you are, and allow your actions to speak for you. Once again, all they have to do is examine your fruit. Another word for fruit is actions. The actions that you produce are good indicators of what you truly believe. Remember, our words mean nothing without the lifestyle to back them up.

Observe your life to see if you're actually living out your beliefs. You don't want to be perceived as a fraud; people will consider you a joke, and you'll become an object of ridicule. This affects your witness and your influence on others. So, be mindful of your conduct at all times, and make sure it corresponds with your words. When you excel in every area of your life, you influence others to do the same. Our goal should be to motivate people to uphold high standards, and not settle for average. It's time to arise!

MEDIOCRITY

Refuse to do the bare minimum. Why be average when you can be great? A person of excellence rejects average and continually strives to be extraordinary. I'm not saying that average is terrible, but if you can do better, then why not do it. Many individuals have settled to be mediocre by not rising above the status quo. This is very disappointing. One of the things that I've observed is that people who are average do just enough to get by. They do what is required of them and nothing more. They refuse to go the extra mile and challenge themselves to greater heights. It's time we challenge ourselves and arise out of our comfort zones. I agree with the statement that says, "Get comfortable with being uncomfortable." This is the only way we're going to realize our true potential. Growth is impossible if you're not challenged in some way or another.

To see growth in our lives, we must resist the path of least resistance. Challenge yourself. Be willing to travel down the more difficult road at times. Only a few people choose to explore the more challenging road or the narrow path. Generally, we prefer to journey the broad path because it seems easier. And we notice that everyone else is drifting that way. On the broad pathway anything goes. People seem to do as they please with no regard of morals and standards. This road leads to destruction. **Matthew 7:13** contends, *"Enter by the narrow gate; for wide is the gate and broad is the way that leads to destruction, and there are many who go in by it. Because narrow is the gate and difficult is the way which leads to life, and there are few who find it."*

Since the broad road doesn't require much effort, it will not produce extraordinary results. If you're not careful, the easier path can lead you to places that you'll later regret. Remember, just because everyone else is doing it, doesn't mean it's the right thing to do. There are more benefits on the narrow path. Once you overcome the challenges, there are great rewards. The rewards always outweigh the trial. For example, let's say you decide to live a healthy lifestyle. Even though its challenging to eat healthy foods and exercise, the reward exceeds the hard work. You gain better health, more energy, higher self-esteem, and more confidence. I say this is worth the challenge. The narrow path compels us to be self-disciplined. It dares us to operate above average. Let's be honest: not everyone is willing to function on that level.

Operating on a higher level will cost you some blood, sweat, and tears, but it's worth it. The rewards are great. An average person is usually content with the status quo and sees no need to reach higher. Now, I'm not saying that they don't desire more, but they're not willing to put in the work that is necessary to become great. Theodore Roosevelt, an author and 26th President of the United States, asserted, "Nothing in this world is worth having or worth doing unless it means effort, pain, and difficulty. No kind of life is worth leading if it's always an easy life..." Anything in life that's valuable and worth pursuing will cost you something. So, expect to pay the bill if you desire greatness.

Think about this. If everything you desired came easy, you wouldn't really appreciate it because it didn't cost you anything. You didn't have to work for it. For example, let's say your son is in college and all of his friends have cars. Now he communicates to you that he wants a car as well. You notice that most of his friend's parents purchased their vehicles and they didn't have to work for them. As a result, his friends don't value what's been given to them. They take it for granted. These friends don't wash the cars, change the oil, nor do they perform the normal maintenance duties. The reason they don't value the gift is due to no investment on their part; they didn't have to work for it. And since they didn't have to work for the vehicles, there is no appreciation.

On the other hand, your son has been saving up his money and finally has enough to buy him a used car. His attitude towards his vehicle is entirely different from his friends. He had to save, sacrifice, and invest his savings to get this car; therefore, he appreciates the vehicle. He values his car. He knows the sacrifices he made to purchase that car, and that's why he refuses to take it for granted. This car means more to your son because it cost him something. We must be willing to put in the time and effort for the things that we desire. Once we do, our lives will never be the same. We will soar to greater heights.

One of the things I've realized is that when you challenge yourself, you'll achieve things that you've never imagined you could accomplish. You will surprise yourself. How can you know what you're capable of if you never try? I really do believe that some of us are unaware of our real potential; we have no idea of what we're capable of achieving. For instance, when I decided to enroll back in school, it was terrifying for me. I remember thinking to myself, "Can I do this?" I doubted whether or not I could write a thirty-page paper. The thought of writing a paper of this magnitude frightened me at my core; however, this was the challenge set before me.

When I completed this paper, I was so amazed and proud of what I had accomplished. In the beginning, I didn't believe that I was capable of achieving this task, especially since I never enjoyed writing in the past. I was determined to stretch myself, and as a result, I finished the paper. And now I have more confidence in my abilities than ever before.

Let me share another example. In 2016 I had this overwhelming desire to do a Women's Conference for 2017, but I was afraid. I had no previous experience; I had never done a conference before. And honestly, it was terrifying. I didn't know where to start. But I did it, despite my fear. I stepped out in faith, and now I'm preparing for my third conference for 2019. So, from this experience, I can advise you to just go for it. Whatever goals and dreams you desire to accomplish, it's time to reach for them. Yes, you may fail at times, but that doesn't mean that you are a failure. When you give up and stop trying, then you become a failure.

Examine yourself and identify the things that are keeping you from reaching your full potential. It could be fear, low self-esteem, relationships, or your current job situation. Once you've identified the hindrance, make an effort to overcome that stumbling block. You need to adopt an "I can do this" mentality. Believe that you can accomplish your hopes and dreams. Never allow anyone to tell you that you can't do it. Prove to yourself that have what it takes. You have so much treasure hidden on the inside of you that's waiting to be discovered. Tap into it. The world needs what you have to offer. Step out in faith and pursue your dreams. There is so much more to you than you realize.

INTEGRITY

There are certain qualities that you must possess if you're going to live an extraordinary existence. One of those qualities is integrity. People with integrity are honest, upright, and authentic. They say what they mean and mean what they say. When you're an honest individual, you tend to be consistent in your words and deeds. You refuse to live a dual existence. Your actions in public are consistent with your private behavior because you know God sees all things. If our conduct behind closed doors is not in line with what we are portraying to the public, we are living a double life. And everything that's hidden will eventually be exposed; what's done in the dark will be brought to light (**Matt. 6:4**). Wow, this is the truth!

When I was younger, I remember trying to hide certain things from my grandmother, but she would eventually discover the truth. My secret never remained a secret forever. Whether you believe someone is watching or not, your deeds will be made known. Now, remember, this works both ways. If you're doing good deeds privately, God will openly reward you. The Bible points out, "...*thy Father which seeth in secret himself shall reward thee openly*" (**Matthew 6:4**). So good or bad, all of your secret deeds will eventually be revealed. Once again, our heavenly Father sees it all. And if we're not aware of this, then we'll continue to fall short of excellence.

Decide to become a person of excellence. Always strive to keep a clear conscience toward God and others. And to do this, you must maintain integrity in all of your affairs. Remain honorable in everything you do. Try your best to treat others like you would like to be treated because we do reap what we sow. Monitor your thoughts, and constantly be aware of what you speak to others; words are powerful. Words can uplift a person or destroy them. If we desire to walk in honor and excellence, we must attempt to respect, value, and inspire everyone we encounter.

Our goal is to exhibit integrity everywhere we go such as work, school, home, church, and among friends. Yes, we will fall short, but that's okay. At least you are trying. Some people don't even try to improve their life. If you fail, learn the lesson from that experience, and attempt to do better the next time. When you do this, it shows your willingness to grow and develop as a person.

Be open to instruction, and stay ready to accept correction from others. It takes a strong person to admit when they're wrong. This requires humility and a teachable spirit. You must be willing to accept constructive criticism if you desire to become a person of excellence. Pride hinders your growth. There are no benefits to walking in pride. Learn to acknowledge your faults. Confront your weak areas and decide to make changes. You can't change what you are unwilling to confront. Being honest with yourself creates room for growth, which allows you to soar to greater heights.

Take advice from others, and stop pretending that you know it all because you don't. You don't know what you don't know. There is nothing attractive about a person that thinks they know everything. It's actually annoying. A "know it all" person possesses a prideful attitude that will eventually lead them down a dangerous path. These types of individuals are usually self-absorbed and egotistical. **Proverbs 18:12** warns us that pride comes before destruction, so please take heed. A prideful attitude will keep you from growing and excelling in life.

If there is a situation that warrants your apology, then go apologize, whether you feel like it or not. Our feelings should never dictate our actions. The decision to apologize is not a matter of feelings; it's a matter of doing the right thing. There have been times when I've been prompted in my heart to apologize to someone even though I wasn't the person at fault. But it doesn't matter who was wrong. If God impresses on your heart for you to apologize, then do it. This is a test of humility, and sometimes it's necessary to maintain harmony.

Ask yourself. Is being right more important than keeping a great friendship? Do you only apologize when you feel you are in the wrong? Apologizing doesn't mean that you're wrong, weak, or timid; it suggests that you're willing to humble yourself and do whatever is necessary to salvage the relationship and keep the peace. God will test us sometimes, so be ready. The Bible admonishes us to seek peace, and work to maintain it (**Psalms 34:14**). Seeking peace does not mean you have to compromise on your beliefs or shy away from your convictions. It's not about that; instead, it's about maintaining a Christ-like attitude and influencing others to do the same. Make decisions that advocate peace without compromising your core values.

COMPROMISE

Compromising doesn't always suggest that a person is disregarding God's principles and their own convictions for the sake of others. Compromising also means a settlement of differences in which both parties make allowances for each other. There will be times in our lives when we'll have to compromise in our relationships. Once again, as long as you're not disobeying God's principles, then it's okay. For example, you and a friend are trying to decide where to eat Friday night. You desire pizza, and she is craving hamburgers. You chose the last restaurant you all dined at; therefore, it's your turn to compromise and allow your friend to pick her restaurant of choice this time. It's the right thing to do. Yes, you are compromising, but not at the expense of your own values and convictions.

A person of excellence will strive to meet others halfway. If possible, they will make decisions that are beneficial for all parties involved. Just remember, we never compromise the truth to gain favor or promotion from others. Our increase comes from God. He is our main source, and everything else is just a resource that He has provided for us. The Bible teaches us that our promotions do not come from the east, west, nor the south, but it is God who judges. He determines who will rise and who will fall **(Psalms 75: 6-7)**. God has the power to enlarge our territories without us compromising our values. We must remain obedient to His teachings and refuse to waiver.

Know your boundaries and stay true to your convictions. If you fall, view it as a teachable moment, and gain the necessary information for you to grow and succeed in life. Just because we fall at times doesn't mean we're failures. Failure is when you decide to throw in the towel and never try again. No one is without fault, so learn the lesson and move forward. Richelle E. Goodrich, an American author, and novelist states, "Many times what we perceive as an error or failure is actually a gift. And eventually we find that lessons learned from that discouraging experience prove to be of great worth." There's always wisdom to be gained from every experience in life. Continue to stand firm for the truth no matter what, and you'll excel in every area of your life.

Questions for Discussion & Reflection:

1. After reading this chapter, what insight did you gain as it relates to developing the spirit of excellence?

2. What is excellence? What does it look like to you? Explain.

3. Do you operate in excellence? Do you go above and beyond the call of duty? If not, why?

4. Are you a committed and dependable person? What are your weak areas?

5. What is mediocrity? When was the last time you moved out of your comfort zone? Please explain.

6. Identify the areas in your life that are hindering you from becoming a person of excellence. What are some steps you can take to improve in these areas?

7. What is integrity? Are you a person of integrity?

Next Level Living

CHAPTER 11

LEARNING CONTENTMENT

Are you content in your current season? Or are you restless and dissatisfied with your progress in life? Contentment is being satisfied to the point where you are not disturbed, no matter what's going on. It's being pleased with who you are and what you have in the current season, knowing that you are growing and making progress. Contentment doesn't mean you stand still and do nothing until something happens. No, you need to be diligently working toward your goals while patiently awaiting your breakthrough.

We must be willing to endure the process that God takes us through if we plan on moving to the next level. There will be seasons that are uncomfortable and challenging, but they are all necessary for our development. Learn how to be content in every phase of your life, and recognize that it's only temporary. Circumstances don't last forever; they're just for a season. In the New Testament, the writer Paul states,

> *"Not that I speak in regard to need, for I have learned in whatever state I am, to be content: I*

know how to be abased, and I know how to abound.
Everywhere and in all things I have learned both to
be full and to be hungry, both to abound and to
suffer need. I can do all things through Christ who
*strengthens me (**Philippians 4:11-13**).*

The writer Paul is expressing how he learned how to be content in whatever situation or season he was experiencing. He learned how to be satisfied in the good and the bad times because he understood that circumstances do change. They are short-lived. We should learn to do this as well. Our lives would be much more joyous and peaceful if we altered our perspectives about the situations we face in life. Remember, it's only for a season!

PERSPECTIVE

How do you view your current situations? You may need to change your perspective. Your circumstance is only a problem if you view it as a problem. Start seeing your challenging times as opportunities to gain knowledge and develop. You'll be amazed at how content you become when you take on that perspective. When you decide to be content in your current season, it allows you to learn, grow, persist, and embrace the present season. It's all about how you look at your experiences.

Now, I'm not saying that we're not hurt or pained by certain circumstances, but I am saying that we need to view that situation as a small piece of a bigger picture. Focus on the vision that you have for your life, and keep everything in perspective. Remember, you're not going to be there forever. Just concentrate on the things that are going well, and refuse to stress about things you have no control over. If you can do something about the situation, then do it. If not, release it to God and focus on doing the things you have control over.

How you manage this season will dictate your blessings for the next season. Make sure you keep the right attitude toward your present circumstances. Learn to be thankful for what you have, and worry less about what you don't have. If you only have a little, be content with the little as you work toward more. Keep working and keep growing. God will add more to your life when He sees that you are devoted to improving what you already have. Why should God bless you with more if you're discontented and unfaithful with the resources you've been given. Be committed to the people, assignments, and opportunities that He has already blessed you with. When you do this, expect to receive an increase. God is watching your faithfulness.

When God sees that you have been faithful over a few things, He will make you are leader over many more things (**Matthew 25:23**). Make an effort to be a good steward over what you currently have, and watch how your life attracts increase. Don't frown on small beginnings. Just do the best you can with what you have because everything starts small. If you persist and never give up, you will eventually see significant progress. Just stay humble. Humility compels you to be thankful for what you have and not walk around with a sense of entitlement. It also requires you to be patient, and when you are patient, you'll keep doing the work until you see increase no matter how long it takes.

HUMILITY

Contentment requires you to be humble. When you walk in humility, you tend to be more grateful for the people and things that are in your life. You don't take it for granted. A humble person appreciates every season that God has allowed them to experience. They refuse to murmur and complain when things are not going their way. Also, a humble person understands that seasons come, and seasons go, but God will always be with them and see them through.

In my challenging seasons, I would always say, "This too shall pass." This basically means that the situation is not here to stay, and it will eventually move on. However, you must ask yourself, what have I gained from this? We shouldn't miss the opportunity to acquire the insight we need to operate in the next phase of our lives. There's always wisdom to be extracted from trying times if we just pay attention. Everything we've learned in the previous seasons will be vital in the following seasons. So, humble yourself, and learn the lessons.

Every experience can be seen as a teachable moment, but if we're too proud, we'll miss the opportunity to learn what we need from that experience. An individual with a prideful attitude is never satisfied or content with their lives. They usually resent their challenging seasons and become consumed with trying to fix everything. We must understand that some circumstances are out of our control and beyond our skill set. If we remain prideful, we'll try to fix and repair every trial that transpires in our life; even though we need to surrender those situations over to God.

In some situations, you have to do what you can and leave the rest for God to settle. Be content and wait on God. Please don't misunderstand me. I don't believe we should be satisfied with living a mediocre existence nor do I believe we should settle for less than God's best for us. Yes, we should maintain a desire to achieve more and grow more; however, we also must learn how to be content with each stage of our journey. Every level that God promotes us to should be experienced with a heart of gratitude and contentment.

People who maintain an arrogant attitude will delay their progress and hinder their growth. God doesn't promote pride. Favor will be shown to you if you remain humble. **1 Peter 5:5** teaches, "...*all of you be subject one to another, and be clothed with humility: for God resist the proud, and giveth grace to the humble*." Individuals who lack contentment and humility in their lives are usually unhappy with themselves, and they tend to live a shallow existence. These individuals are looking for joy in all the wrong places.

Majority of people who are not content with their lives are seeking joy from external things. Joy comes from within. Create your own happiness, and stop looking to others to make you happy; it's not their responsibility. True fulfillment produces joy, which can only be found in God. No person or thing can totally fulfill you. I believe that we have this God-sized hole in our souls that can only be filled by God. And when He is not allowed to fill it, that place that is designated for Him remains empty and void. Remember, people and things will only provide you with temporary satisfaction, but it'll never be long-lasting. That hole in our souls is meant to be filled by God and God alone. When we attempt to fill that hole with substitutes, we'll always be unfulfilled.

Often, we attempt to find fulfillment in addictions, sex, toxic relationships, titles, power, and wealth, but those things will never satisfy us permanently. Once you establish a relationship with God and allow Him to complete you, you'll begin to experience true happiness. In **John 4:14**, Jesus states to the woman at the well, "…*whoever drinks of the water that I shall give him shall never thirst again, but the water that I shall give him shall become a well of water springing up in him for eternal life.*"

I love this verse. This text is saying that we must go to Jesus to be fulfilled. Our souls thirst and yearn for something so much deeper than any human being can provide. We were made to need and depend on God.

John Piper, an American pastor, author, and chancellor of Bethlehem College & Seminary insisted, "The deepest and most enduring happiness is found only in God. Not from God, but in God." Until we get a revelation of this and begin to seek God for fulfillment, our lives will feel empty. Focus your thoughts on God; remain grateful for all He's done for you, and you'll begin to experience contentment in your heart and soul. It all starts with your thinking.

RIGHT THINKING

Contentment is developed in your life when you maintain the right mindset. Instead of always thinking about what you need and what you lack, decide to be a blessing to someone else. Realize that God wants to use you in this season. Begin to look for ways to serve Him. Just because this season of your life is not progressing the way you want it to, doesn't mean that you're not where God wants you to be. Exercise some patience. Figure out what you must do to be of service to others, and do it. Once you do this, I promise you will see joy manifest in your life.

Think of all the opportunities and lessons that we miss when our minds are consumed with discontentment. When you think on all the blessings that God has bestowed upon your life, it should produce a feeling of contentment in your soul. The Bible reminds us that a man becomes what he thinks in his heart (**Proverbs 23:7**). You will eventually become the thoughts you continuously meditate on. If you keep thinking about certain things long enough, you will sooner or later act out those thoughts. This is why it's so important for us to monitor our thinking. Our job is to cast down any ideas and imaginations that are contrary to the knowledge of God, and replace those thoughts with the truth (**2 Corinthians 10:5**). Renew your thinking!

Feelings of discontentment can cause us to make unwise decisions. Discontentment produces impatience. If you're not careful, you will jump ahead of God and begin to pursue things that you're not quite ready for in this season. Anything that is received prematurely can be harmful to you. Blessings and promotions without spiritual growth can be damaging for you and the people attached to you. God will never promote you prematurely. Wait on God. Be content as you allow Him to work in you and mature you. Once God has developed you, you'll be equipped to handle the promotions that He desires to give you.

For instance, let's say you've decided that you need to improve your money managing skills. You are horrible at budgeting, and you tend to squander money on unnecessary items. Currently, you have committed to grow in this area of your life. You're working on budgeting techniques and ways to save more money monthly; however, you're still a work in progress. You still need to grow more in this area. Well, God is not going to bless and prosper your finances right now because He knows you're not ready for that level of responsibility. Providing you with an abundance of money in this season would be more of a curse than a blessing. Remember, God doesn't promote us prematurely.

So, why would a premature promotion be more of a curse than a blessing? Well, if God increased your finances before you're able to manage that responsibility, more than likely you would mismanage the funds and engage in frivolous spending because you're not prepared to handle that level of blessings. Again, it would do more harm than good, and later cause you great disappointment. We must stop expecting to receive more than we're prepared for. Make sure you have reasonable expectations. If you know you're not equipped for something, ask God to prepare you, so that you can be in a position to receive the promotion when it's your time. Learn to manage your expectations!

MANAGING YOUR EXPECTATIONS

There's nothing wrong with having expectations, but we must avoid misplaced expectations. When we place an expectation on someone who is incapable of satisfying our needs, we are misplacing our expectations. Also, when we expect people to do for us what only God can do— we are misplacing our expectations. I know we all have expectations in life; however, we must be reasonable and sober about our expectation of others because misplaced expectations will eventually cause us some great disappointments. Of course, we'll all experience some disappointments in life, but we can also dodge some of these regrets by managing our expectations.

Make sure you are preparing yourself for the things that you are expecting to manifest in your life. I like to say, "Preparation precedes expectation." Once again, prepare for what you are expecting. God doesn't grant us what we want; he gives us what we prepare for. For example, you have a vision that you're going to be a transformational speaker, helping people all over the world to transform their lives. Since this is what you are expecting to manifest in your life, you must begin to prepare. Place yourself in a position for this to happen. Do what you can do, and God will do the rest.

Remember, there's always a season of preparation. So, if you desire to be a transformational speaker, you must be willing to endure the training process before your speaking dream is achieved. During the preparation period, you need to be refining your communication skills and developing your vocabulary. Also, you would need to practice speaking in front of people as much as possible. Any opportunity you receive to speak, you should probably take it, unless you don't feel peace about it. If you continue to work diligently on improving your talents and skills, opportunities will materialize— guaranteed.

Make sure you understand that some people will disappoint you and fail to follow through on their promises. Unfortunately, many individuals lack the integrity to keep their word, so be prepared for this. We must not allow other people's inconsistencies to dictate our attitudes. Your attitude belongs to you, and you have the power to control it. Tame your reactions, think before you respond, and continuously check your expectations.

UNMET EXPECTATIONS

Unmet expectations by others have the potential to leave you bitter, angry, depressed, and resentful; that's why you should try your best to maintain reasonable expectations. Is it possible that the source of your anger is derived from unmet expectations? Did someone promise to do something for you and failed to deliver? Well, we've all experienced this at some point in our lives. People experience this in marriages, friendships, businesses, and with acquaintances. There is no way around disappointments because we're all human. And human beings will disappoint us occasionally. When we're in a relationship with others, there is a level of expectation we have from them. Just make sure it's reasonable, or you will set yourself up for a letdown.

Oftentimes, we have too much faith and trust in people. Remember, we're imperfect human beings. And people are destined to fail us at some point. That's why the Bible warns, "*It is better to trust in the Lord than to put confidence in man* (**Psalms 118:8**)." Place your expectations in God, and you'll never be disappointed. I truly believe if we're not careful, we'll expect things from people who can't live up to our expectations. They just cannot deliver. And it's really not fair to the other person because we're expecting something from them that's possibly beyond their ability.

Living up to other people's expectations can be challenging. Especially, when they expect you to become who they think you should be. We only can be who God created us to be. So, when other people try to mold you into someone who God never intended for you to become, it can be very frustrating. We must learn to accept people for who they are and who God made them to be. Just because you expect an individual to behave in a particular manner doesn't mean they will comply. This is what you expect from them, but it may not be who they are. Manage your expectations.

The problem arises when we place our unwanted expectations on individuals, and they fail to meet those expectations. Now we're upset and disappointed in them, but they never agreed to live up to our expectations in the first place. This usually occurs among friends, acquaintances, and family members. The hurt and disappointment that we feel are self-inflicted because these were our hopes and not theirs. Unmet expectations can affect your relationship with the people you love. Just make sure you're not misplacing your expectations— and if you are— you're putting yourself at risk of getting hurt.

When you perform a generous act for someone, do you always expect something in return from that individual? If so, it's unwise because you're setting yourself up for disappointment. Check your motives. If you're offering a gift or providing a service from your heart, then there is no need to expect them to return the favor. I agree with the anonymous quote that says, "If you're helping someone and expecting something in return, you're doing business, not kindness." Experience the freedom of giving without expectation.

Avoid reminding a person of all the good deeds you've done for them, especially when you're asking for their help. When you do this, it's an indication that your good deeds were not sincerely given from the heart. Remember that God sees all things, and He will compensate you. The Bible states, *"God will repay each person according to what they have done"* (**Romans 2:6**). You will always reap what you sow; therefore, if you plant good seeds toward others, God will make sure you reap a good harvest. Expect God to do for you what others fail to do. Trust Him to take care of you.

TRUSTING GOD

When your faith is entirely in God, you believe that He is working behind the scenes on your behalf during difficult times. Lack of trust will cause you to be discontent. For example, let's say you have a vision for your life, and you're working on it every day. There are days that you question whether or not this vision will come to pass. Sometimes you have doubt, but you continue to push forward—despite what you feel. If this vision is from God, and you refuse to trust Him to help you manifest the vision, it will cause you irritation, discontentment, and anger. You'll begin to feel like you have to make the vision come to pass on your own, and this is not true. Whatever vision God has given you, He will help establish that vision and provide the necessary resources to make it happen; but you must trust that He will do it.

God will give you provision for His vision. You may not understand how He's going to do it, but that's not your concern.

Don't worry about the 'how' just focus on the 'what.' Your job is to trust in God with all your heart and lean not to your own understanding. When you do this, He will direct your paths (**Prov. 3:5-6**). Yes, I know this can be challenging at times, but the more you do it, the better you become at trusting God.

Trusting in God means you believe that He has a good plan for your future, and you're willing to obey Him. It means you may not know every detail of that plan, but you trust Him anyway. Now, I know we dislike not knowing all the details of God's purpose for our lives, but we trust that He knows exactly what He is doing. He's working everything together for our good. Do you believe this? Are you confident that God will help you to fulfill your purpose in life? If not, you will live in fear, doubt, and discontentment. This is not God's desire for us. Sometimes we desire to know things that God is not ready to reveal to us. He will reveal everything we need to know in due season; be satisfied with that.

Learn how to be content in every season of your life. If you're going to grow and fulfill your purpose, you must be willing to endure the process. This journey requires us to be content in every phase of life; otherwise, we'll get impatient and attempt to sidestep the process. This could really set us back; so be patient. Prepare to go through the development stages. And when you do this, you'll reach your destiny.

Questions for Discussion & Reflection:

1. After reading this chapter, what insight did you gain as it relates to learning contentment?

2. What is contentment? Are you content in your current season? If not, why?

3. How can your perspective change the way you feel about a challenging season?

4. What are misplaced expectations? Do you have misplaced expectations? Are your expectations in God?

5. How can you better manage your expectations?

6. Do you have faith in God? Do you trust Him with your future?

7. How can trusting God help you to fulfill your purpose in life?

CHAPTER 12

OVERCOMING TEMPTATIONS AND WEAKNESSES

Everyone struggles with temptations because it's a part of everyday life. We're all tempted in one way or another. According to Oxford Dictionaries, temptation is defined as a strong desire to do something, especially something wrong or unwise. It's a certain pull or enticement that usually leads to immoral actions. There are many ways in which we are tempted daily. For example, we get tempted to stay offended, unforgiving, worry, overeat, lie, stay angry, complain, and seek revenge. Temptations usually thrive on our weaknesses; therefore, it's vital that we identify our weak points.

We're typically tempted by the things we lust after; it's difficult to be lured by something you have no desire for. If I don't want it, it's hard to tempt me with it. The Bible warns, *"But each one is tempted when he is drawn away by his own desires and enticed. Then, when desire has conceived, it gives birth to sin; and sin, when it is full-grown, brings forth death"* (**James 1:14-15**). We are commonly tempted in our areas of weakness.

191

PERSONAL WEAKNESSES

What are your vulnerabilities? Everyone has weaknesses. Some of us try to hide our shortcomings or deceive ourselves by not admitting that we have them. Just because we don't admit we have flaws doesn't mean they're not there. When you identify your weak areas, you have a higher chance of overcoming the temptations that seem to defeat you continually. Majority of Christians believe that admitting their weaknesses will cause people to respect them less as a Christian, but this is not the case. People will respect you more when you are truthful about who you are, so don't be afraid to identify your weak areas. Acknowledging your weaknesses doesn't mean something is wrong with you; it just says that you are aware of your flaws and you have a desire to correct them. Remember, we are human, and we all have imperfections.

I have no problem with admitting my flaws, and I'm quite familiar with my weak areas— one of them being impatience. I can be very intolerant when things don't work out according to plan. Also, I tend to want things to happen right now, and I rarely like to wait. My impatience has caused plenty of challenges in my life, including financial issues, relationships, and health problems. Because I'm tempted to get extremely impatient at times, I put forth extra effort to resist that urge. I try to exercise patience on purpose. I've gotten better over time, but I still struggle with it occasionally. It's a process.

Overcoming our weaknesses is an ongoing process. It's never-ending. We'll always be tempted by something until the day we die, but we'll continue to overcome. The key is understanding that we can't do it by ourselves. Our weaknesses will not be defeated in our own abilities. We need help. The grace of God helps us to overcome any temptations or difficulties we face in life. However, we must humble ourselves and acknowledge that we're incapable of overcoming these enticements in our own strength. Sometimes the temptation is so strong that we need divine help to overpower it.

When we humble ourselves, we open the door for God's grace to enter and operate in our lives. His grace shows up in our weakest moments. God's grace is sufficient; it is made perfect in our weaknesses (**2 Corinthians 12:9-10**). God's strength and power allow us to overcome every test, trial, and tribulation that we encounter in life. Just remember, you are not alone in your battles. Whatever infirmities or weaknesses you face today, someone else has faced them and got the victory. Your situation is not uncommon to humanity. It will not defeat you.

COMMON TO MAN

Majority of the temptations we face are common to the human race, such as pride, lust, greed, power, sexual immorality, and complaining. We must be on guard against these temptations. Stand firm in the faith and resist the urge to give in to your weaknesses. God never promised that we would never be tempted, but He did promise to give us the power to overcome it. God will also provide us a way of escape. According to **1 Corinthians 10:13**, *"There hath no temptation taken you but such as is common to man: but God is faithful, who will not suffer you to be tempted above that ye are able; but will with the temptation also make a way to escape, that ye may be able to bear it."*

This text reminds us that no one has a special circumstance. Someone in the world has been tempted by the very same thing you're struggling with today, but the great news is that they overcame, and so can you. Knowing that somebody else has defeated a similar situation as you should be very encouraging. This should give you a sense of hope, and motivate you to press through whatever dilemma you're facing on today. If God helped others to conquer, He would help you to overcome all the same. God does not show favoritism (**Acts 10:34**).

Remember, the temptations we face are usually aimed at our weaknesses. For example, formerly I was an impulsive buyer.

I never considered the price of my purchases. If I wanted something, I bought it; no question about it. This cost me dearly later in life. My finances suffered greatly because I never counted the cost. Now, I know better, and I currently attempt to take preventative measures. If I know I have an event coming up in a month or so, I go ahead and start searching for my attire ahead of time, hoping to find a bargain. This prevents last minute shopping, which usually leads to impulsive buying and overspending. Refuse to give in to your unhealthy appetites because they will eventually destroy you. Temptations are not to be taken lightly. When you're feeling weak, pray to God for the grace you need to overcome. Learn how to resist these cravings and exercise some self-control.

RESIST

The more you indulge in your weaknesses, the more you'll crave them. Whatever you feed grows. And when you continue to feed bad habits, you'll eventually develop a larger appetite for them. This will ultimately ruin you. Those bad habits will become addictions that will begin to shape your thinking and behavior. Before you know it, you're in bondage to these destructive habits. They now control you. You're now a slave to these addictions because whatever controls you, dominates your life. Refuse to become enslaved to harmful habits. **Romans 6:16** teaches, *"Don't you realize that you become the slave of whatever you choose to obey? You can be a slave to sin, which leads to death, or you can* *choose to obey God, which leads to righteous living.*" This text is saying if we choose to obey immorality, we become a slave to that evil, which leads to a life of destruction; but if we choose to obey God, it produces a blessed life. I choose the blessed life.

There was a time when I chose a destructive lifestyle. It all started when I was around sixteen years of age and continued until I was about thirty-one. I remember back during my college years, I continuously engaged in heavy alcohol drinking, recreational drugs, and other destructive activities. I was having much fun— so I thought. I continued to give in to my temptations to drink alcohol and indulge in other self-destructive behaviors. At the time, I didn't realize that alcohol was a weakness that I possessed. So, my fun turned into a habit, habit turned into an addiction, and addiction turned into bondage. Years had passed, and I was now in bondage to these addictions. I was no longer in control. The bad habits that I thought I once controlled were now controlling me. These addictions had overpowered my life. Now, everything I engaged in centered around those awful habits.

I finally surrendered and acknowledged that I couldn't defeat these addictions on my own, so I invited God into my life to help me. My pain forced me to seek God. He empowered me to overcome my addictions, and now I'm free from all of those poor habits— that once kept me shackled. The strongholds have been broken off of my life. I no longer entertain any of these temptations because now I understand that they have the potential to destroy me and kill my hopes and dreams.

Remember, being tempted is not a sin. Temptation only becomes a sin when you surrender to it. When we're tempted, we have a choice to do it God's way or our own way. Our method is usually not the best way. *"There is a way which seemeth right unto a man, but the end thereof are the ways of death"* (**Proverbs 14:12**).

GOD'S ESCAPE

So, what do we do when we feel tempted to get revenge or stay angry? In order to escape temptation, we must follow God's principles. If we just trust God, His teachings will always provide us with a solution when we're faced with temptation. For example, when someone has offended you, and you are tempted to seek revenge, I urge you to trust God's word that says, *do not seek revenge, but leave room for God's anger. Vengeance is mine; I will repay, says the Lord.* (**Romans 12:19**). Allow God to handle the offense, and refuse to stoop to their level. If you decide to seek revenge, then you set yourself up to reap what you sow. Don't do it. Uphold your standards.

You may be tempted to complain and murmur about some things that are happening or not happening in your life. This could be a sign of discontentment. Guard against this, and choose to be content. Complaining about your current circumstances will not help your life. It only makes the situation worse because it robs you of your present joy and peace. It's not worth it. Focus on what you can do to help the situation, and surrender the rest over to God. Allow Him to help you do what only He can do. There will always be issues that seem to be out of our control, so don't stress about it; pray about it. And watch God work. Remember, your circumstances are seasonal. They don't last forever.

Trust that God will supply your needs and provide a way of escape when you're tempted to indulge in sinful or immoral behavior. **1 Corinthians 10:13** insists, *…but God is faithful, who will not suffer you to be tempted above that ye are able; but will with the temptation also make a way to escape, that ye may be able to bear it.*" Have you ever been tempted to indulge in sexual immorality? Well, I'm sure we've all been tempted with this at some point in our lives. One of the ways to escape "sexual immorality" is by taking a moment to consider the consequences.

We're often deceived by believing we can sow without reaping. There are always consequences to our actions—good or bad. Participating in sexual immorality can cause sexually transmitted diseases, loss of self-respect, and unwanted pregnancy. It also grieves the heart of God and weakens the faith of those we influence. When specific cravings arise, look for the promises of God. Don't trust your own judgment; seek the truth. Refuse to give in to the temptations of life. Take a stand. Choose to endure and follow God's approach. His way is always the best way!

ENDURANCE

Learn how to control your impulses. Once again, they're a part of everyday life. Everyone struggles with forbidden desires. The more you resist them, the stronger you become, and the more likely you are to conquer those lustful cravings. In this life, you'll be tested and tried; however, you must withstand. We have to remain faithful as we go through sufferings, persecutions, trials, and false accusations. When people persecute us, we're tempted to fight back and repay evil with evil. But Jesus teaches, "...*Love your enemies, bless them that curse you, do good to them that hate you, and pray for them which despitefully use you, and persecute you...*" (**Matthew 5:44**). This is how you grow and gain the victory in your life. Temptations are not always bad. They give you an opportunity to do the right thing. And when you make the right choices in life, it builds your confidence and increases your endurance.

I know we don't like to admit it, but we all need resistance in life. Resistance is required to grow and develop your faith muscles. The more you deny and resist temptations, the more you grow in character. Spiritual maturity is taking place. We all must grow spiritually to reach our maximum potential. If you refuse to grow spiritually, you deny your next level. For instance, when you go to the gym and do resistance training, you are trying to develop your leg and arm muscles. Without resistance training, you will never be able to grow those muscles. Well, apply the same principle to your faith.

You must exercise your faith muscles for those muscles to increase. How do you know your faith is real if it's never tested? How can you test your faith without resistance and adversity? If you want greater faith for greater trials, then your faith must be exercised. Tests and trials are a way to develop your faith. The higher you go in life, the more faith you will need. I've learned that great battles can produce great victories.

Enduring temptations are a part of the faith walk, so get accustomed to it. We're supposed to gain wisdom and maturity after we've been tried and tested. **James 1:2-4** reads, "*My brethren, count it all joy when ye fall into divers temptations; knowing this, that the trying of your faith worketh patience. But let patience have her perfect work, that ye may be perfect and entire, wanting nothing.*" The writer is simply saying that your troubles and difficulties will develop your patience and endurance; therefore, you should count it all joy when you're tested in life. Let the trials mature you. They're working for your good. You're winning!

TESTS/TEMPTATIONS

Growth doesn't happen during the good times; it happens when we're challenged and forced out of our comfort zones. We can never predict when the tests will appear. However, we must always be watchful and ready. I found that opposition usually comes right before God is about to do something great in my life or my ministry. Knowing this gives me the strength and the patience I need to endure, despite what I may feel.

Also, I've experienced extreme tests right before a vision has manifested in my life. For instance, God may show me a vision for my future, and then confirm that vision through an individual. While I diligently work on the vision and wait for it to manifest, several tests will come my way attempting to thwart the plan of God for my life. This is a test of my faith; nevertheless, I must hold on to the promise and patiently wait for the manifestation of God's word.

Temptations usually show up during our weakest moments. For example, in Luke 4, we see how Satan approached Jesus in His weakest hour. Jesus had just fasted for 40 days, and He was hungry. Jesus resisted all the temptations, and so can we. The opposition doesn't wait until you feel like being tempted; it usually tempts you when you are weak, tired, discouraged, sick, burned out, offended, and angry. That's when opposition usually strikes;

so, stay alert. **1 Peter 5:8** urges, *"Be sober, be vigilant; because your adversary the devil, as a roaring lion, walketh about, seeking whom he may devour."*

We must pay attention to our lives and be careful not to make impulsive decisions during times of weariness or other emotional distresses. Build relationships with mature individuals that will help you in your time of need and keep you encouraged during your most vulnerable moments. We must pray for each other's weaknesses and offer a helping hand when we can. Recognize that giving in to your temptations can be destructive to your life and also hurtful to those who are connected to you. Don't be deceived; sin is deceptive.

DECEPTION

Temptation alone is not sinful. Once you act on it, it is now sin, and sin has a way of deceiving us. We become deceived when we think that our actions have no consequence. Sadly, some people believe they will never reap what they sow. Boy are they deceived. Maybe not now, but sooner or later you will harvest what you plant. It's a spiritual law. If you're sowing good seeds throughout your life, then there's no need to fear. Just remember that everything we do in life is a seed. The thoughts we think, the words we speak, and the conduct we display are all seeds. That's why it's imperative that we're always aware of how we talk to people and how we treat one another. The Bible explains it this way, *"Be not deceived; God is not mocked: for whatsoever a man soweth, that shall he also reap"* (**Galatians 6:7**). The seeds you sow today will determine the fruit you reap tomorrow.

I've met people who lie, steal, cheat, deceive, and mistreat others, but as soon as something horrific happens in their life, I hear them say, "I don't know why this is happening to me." Most of them seem to have selective memory. And they have no recollection of all the things they have done to other people. I believe they refuse to believe that you actually reap what you sow in life. That's why they are deceived, but there is hope. If they begin to grasp this concept of "sowing and reaping," and decide to do it God's way, a transformation will begin to take place. We'll start to see good fruit in their lives. You can't go wrong when you follow God's principles. Your life is guaranteed to yield good fruit and shift to new levels. Follow God!

Another way in which we are deceived is when we surround ourselves with negative influences and believe it will not affect us. The influences in your life will help shape your character for better or worse. That's why it's critical to be selective in choosing who you will take advice from, and who will be a part of your inner circle. The Bible declares that evil company corrupts good character (**1 Corinthians 15:33**). Please don't underestimate the power of influence.

If you surround yourself with people who operate in excellence and goes beyond the call of duty, then chances are you will begin to conduct your life in the same manner. Their way of living influences your way of existing. Now, if you're around people who lie and steal all the time, chances are you will lie and steal as well. You are being influenced by their behavior whether you believe it or not. The influence is usually subtle and developed over an extended period. Majority of the time we don't even recognize that we're being affected until something upsetting happens. Resist the temptation to keep company with unruly individuals. Spend your time with people who desire to fulfill their God-given purpose. If you allow God to lead your life, He will place the right people in your path at the right time, and they'll assist you on your journey to destiny.

GOD'S HELP

When temptations come, ask God for strength to endure and to show you how to apply His word to that particular situation. He wants to help. Also, make sure you don't intentionally place yourself in a position to be tempted. This is why it's vital that we identify our weaknesses because the enemy will always aim at our weak spots. The word of God is our greatest defense against temptations. **Psalms 119:11** reads, *"Thy word have I hid in mine heart, that I might not sin against thee."* Abide in God's word, and continue to apply it to your everyday struggles. When you dc this, you'll experience victory in every area of your life.

Questions for Discussion & Reflection:

1. After reading this chapter, what insight did you gain as it relates overcoming temptations and weaknesses?

2. What are some of your weaknesses? How can you guard against temptation in these areas?

3. What are some temptations that are common to humanity?

4. What temptations have you overcome lately? What was your strategy?

5. What are some of the ways we can escape temptations? How can God help us with this challenge?

6. How do tests and trials benefit our lives?

7. When does temptation become sin?

8. Who is influencing your life? What are the benefits of surrounding yourself with the right people?

CHAPTER 13

TAMING YOUR TONGUE

Words are powerful. Our words not only affect others, but they affect us as well. We hear and absorb the words that we speak out of our own mouths. And the words we consistently speak will often cause good things or bad things to enter our lives. Choose your words carefully. **Proverbs 18:21** asserts, *"Death and life are in the power of the tongue: and they that love it shall eat the fruit thereof."* Your tongue can produce life or death for you. That's why it's critical for us to be mindful of the words we speak. When our words are used correctly, they can uplift, motivate, educate, and inspire the hearer; however, when we misuse our words, they will do the opposite.

Once again, it's your choice to either build with your words or destroy with your words. We must recognize that we're creating our world by the words we speak daily. God used words to create the world. According to **Hebrews 11:3**, the writer says, *"Through faith, we understand that the worlds were framed by the **word** of God, so that things which are seen were not made of things which do appear."* In this text, we see that God framed the world by his mere words. This demonstrates to us the power of the spoken word.

Refuse to speak anything that you do not desire to come to fruition. Remember, you set the direction for your life with the words you speak.

Could it be things aren't going so well for you because of the words you are continually speaking over your situation? Perhaps you need to start watching what you say. Negative words will produce a negative life; therefore, if you don't want to see it in your life, don't speak it. Avoid perverse talk and unwholesome speech. This kind of language can do more harm than you realize. Remember, the power of life and death is in your tongue. You choose what type of fruit you will produce in your life by the words you speak. Picture the life you want—then make sure your speech is in alignment.

POWER OF WORDS

The tongue is such a powerful force. And if you don't learn to bridle your tongue, it will cause you many regrets in life. People have been devastated by our words, and our words have also strengthened them. The statements we make to others have the potential to create or destroy, build or tear down, protect or condemn. It's our choice. We control the words that come out of our mouths. How are you using your words? Are you using them to uplift others? There are always opportunities for us to use our words to build and encourage other individuals.

For instance, when you encounter someone who is in despair and sees no light at the end of the tunnel, this is your opportunity to speak hope and faith in their life. You have no idea the impact your words will have on them. When you speak words that are filled with love, hope, and encouragement—that individual is inspired and motivated to keep living. They refuse to give up because of the positive words you declared over their life.

Yes, words do matter. Those hope-filled words that you spoke over a person's life could be all they needed to inspire them to keep pressing forward. The right words given at the right time will offer hope to a person who's in despair. *"Pleasant words are as a honeycomb, sweet to the soul, and health to the bones"* (**Proverbs 16:24**). Again, the right words spoken at the right time by the right person can be life-changing.

Never underestimate the power of the spoken word. You may encounter someone who is contemplating suicide or just want to give up on life. This person sees no way out, but after hearing your testimony on how you prevailed, she decided to spare her life. Your testimony changed her entire thought process. This is significant. You just saved someone's life by your spoken words. How powerful is that? That's why it's essential that we consider our words before speaking. Your words could determine whether someone chooses life or death.

THE HEART

The expressions we use daily reveal what's truly going on in our hearts. Our words really do expose our thoughts; therefore, if we think positive thoughts, our speech will be positive and more uplifting as well. It's all connected. A person usually speaks the feelings and beliefs that are stored in their heart—whether it be joy, peace, love, bitterness, hate, or strife. In the Bible, Jesus stated, "...*for out of the abundance of the heart the mouth speaks*" (**Matthew 12:34**). Jesus is saying that we'll speak the things that are planted in our hearts. Whatever you continue to meditate on will eventually come out of your mouth. It all starts with your heart. It's time we take inventory of our souls because whatever is stored in our hearts will eventually roll off of our tongues.

A critical heart produces critical words, and a loving heart produces loving words. It's just that simple. One of the ways we can defend against critical speech is to guard our hearts. Stay mindful of the seeds you allow others to plant in your heart. Also, watch the words you sow into your heart as well. This is vital. To guard your heart, it will require you to monitor your thoughts, meditations, the things you hear, and the things you allow your eyes to see. We must intentionally guard our hearts and minds because our lives are shaped by our thoughts (**Proverbs 4:23**).

Be consciously aware of what you're thinking at all times if possible. And be careful of the people you allow to speak into your life. When you are listening to individuals, you are lending your ears to them, and their words are being planted in your heart. Stay away from negative and critical people as much as possible. If you continue to listen to people that are bitter and critical, then you are allowing them to plant corrupt seeds in your mind. Those seeds will eventually take root in your heart and begin to show up in your words and your behavior.

For instance, let's say you have two co-workers and one of them offends you; however, you choose to overlook her faults. The other co-worker is in your ear gossiping about the matter and continues to advise you to react unpleasantly towards the offender. So now you have this worker who is gossiping and sowing corrupt seeds in your heart day after day, but you don't believe that it's affecting you. You are deceived. Her words are influencing you whether you realize it or not. Eventually, the critical and harsh words that the co-worker sowed into your heart will surface in your attitude towards your colleague. And it usually happens when you least expect it.

Remember the scripture noted earlier that stated, *"out of the abundance of the heart the mouth speaks."* The evil you allowed to be planted in your heart eventually manifested in your attitude and words. Be conscious of what others are speaking into your soul, and also be mindful of what you speak into a person's heart as well. Everything we say is a seed. When you speak, you are planting seeds. So, please continually examine your words, especially when you're in a trial. The words you speak while you're facing hardships could be the difference between victory and defeat. Watch your words.

If you have critical friends who frequently chat about the downfall of others, then you may need to reconsider those relationships. Stay away from individuals that consistently gossip, spread rumors and always talk about hearsay. Run from them. Those are not the kind of conversations you need to be engaged in. Condemning other people is not beneficial to your future nor is it conducive to your growth process. It's a waste of time and energy. Don't allow people to burden you with their negative talk; it only drains you. Refuse to participate in corrupt communication that seeks to destroy others. God does not approve of this; therefore, we must disassociate ourselves from it.

ENCOURAGEMENT

Our words shouldn't damage other people but rather elevate and encourage growth. Learn to speak well of yourself and others also. God desires for our conversations to be pure and disciplined. **Ephesians 4:29** says, *"Let no corrupt communication proceed out of your mouth, but that which is good to the use of* *edifying, that is may minister grace unto the hearers.*" When our words are helpful and wholesome, it influences other people to do the same. It inspires other individuals to be more positive in their approach to life. People will know who you represent by the words you speak and the actions you display. Speak words of truth to enlighten others and help them on their journey. Everyone needs a lift and a helping hand now and again. No one is self-made. You will always need somebody to help you along this journey called life. Every opportunity I get to speak words of encouragement to someone, I take it. It gives me so much joy when I can do so. Learn to speak life!

When you're in a position to inspire and uplift someone, do it. It will give you great joy and satisfaction. Let your words be a fountain of life, whereby others are enriched and stimulated to grow and improve. Always remember that your godly attitude and encouraging words can alter the course of someone's life. That's how important your words are, so use them wisely. Look for opportunities to give hope, and in doing so, your life will be transformed as well. It's a win-win situation.

Did you know that words have the power to remain with people for twenty to fifty years? Yes, I know some individuals who are in their forties and fifties that are still affected by words spoken to them in elementary school. They've never been healed or set free from those words. For example, I know an individual who's fifty-five years old, and at the age of seven, he was told by a school teacher that he would never amount to anything. The teacher said to him, "You are nothing, and you will never be anything." Shocking, I know. Well, this person has never forgotten those words and is still affected by those statements. Many of the issues that this individual struggles with— such as insecurity, rejection, self-hatred, and timidity— stemmed from the treatment of this teacher many years ago. Words are powerful!

Some people seek help and become free from the negative words of others, and some never heal from those wounds. Examine your language regularly, and choose to bring light to dark places with the words that you speak. Learn how to speak God's word over your situations. Remember, He framed the world with His words.

God's word is light, and when you speak it, you're shedding light on your circumstances. The Bible says that Christ followers are the light of the world. So, go and shed some light on this dark world. We are vessels used by God to bring light into dark places. Don't be afraid of the dark. Don't be fearful of godless people. We are here to share the truth with them. You must let your light shine. Hurting people need to see that light.

God wants to share his love with others through us. We are His vessels and to be effectively used by God, we must exercise self-restraint. Discipline your tongue and make sure your words are life-giving. Pay attention to what you say because your words do matter. Always think before you speak.

BRIDLE THE TONGUE

Bridling your tongue can be very difficult at times, but it's necessary. The word "bridle" means to control, hold, restrain, and discipline something. If we're going to serve God and help people, we must learn how to bridle our tongues. Be quick to listen and slow to speak (**James 1:19**). Whenever you have the opportunity to remain silent, do it—especially if it's in your best interest to do so. We're all held accountable for what we say in this lifetime. Just because you think it, doesn't mean you need to say it. We must learn how to use wisdom when we speak. If you desire to grow and reach new levels, learn how to control your tongue. Everything is not meant to be spoken.

In **Matthew 12:36-37** Jesus declares, *"But I say unto you, that every idle word that men shall speak, they shall give account thereof in the day of judgment. For by thy words, thou shalt be justified, and by thy words thou shalt be condemned."* Jesus is telling us that we will be held accountable for every idle word that we speak. Wow! This forces me to be more careful with my words, particularly when I'm upset or angry. I use to think that words didn't matter before I was enlightened about the power of words. I didn't realize how powerful and life-changing the spoken word could be. Now I monitor my words, and I'm careful of what I say to others. I'm more intentional about the words that I speak because I know better. And when you know better, you should do better.

There were times in my life when I was tempted to defend myself with words and actions, but it wasn't beneficial for me. People were falsely accusing me of things I've never done. Knowing that I was innocent made it very difficult for me not to retaliate and try to clear my name of those false accusations. But sometimes we must remain silent. It's not always in our best interest to fight for ourselves. If you know you're doing the right thing, just keep doing it. God sees it all. I like the quote that says, "Sometimes it's best to stay quiet. The silence can speak volumes without ever saying a word."

All the good that you're doing in life will be revealed in due season, whether people acknowledge it or not. You never have to go around explaining yourself or justifying your actions to anyone. When people assault your character, keep quiet, and allow God to fight your battles. *"The Lord shall fight for you, and ye shall hold your peace"* (**Exodus 14:14**). If someone verbally attacks you, that doesn't permit you to assault them back verbally.

Never reduce yourself to someone else's level. Stay on top and let them rise to your level if they decide to do so. We must choose our battles wisely. God instructs us to overcome evil by doing good; therefore, we should refuse to repay evil with evil. Responding the right way will always bring about growth and increase in your life. You may not see it now, but you'll eventually reap good fruit when you choose to do it God's way.

Always try to bring others up to your level. When you encounter unkind and immature individuals, your goal is to influence them to think higher; help them to develop spiritually. In this lifetime, people are going to say things to hurt you, disappoint you, and offend you. However, you must never reduce yourself to their level by speaking hateful things or retaliating. Again, you are accountable for what you say and do. God will avenge us if we just surrender our desire to avenge ourselves.

In the Bible, God says, *"...Vengeance is Mine; I will repay..."* (**Romans 12:19**). When God fights for you, victory is guaranteed. But it's very important that we respond to the controversy the way God instructs us to— if we desire to experience this victory. Learn how to apply Godly principles to your challenging situations. When you do this, you will inevitably experience a favorable outcome. Pray for people instead of fighting back with them. You are fighting a losing battle when you choose to take matters into your own hands. Remember, God commanded us to love one another, not fight each other.

Yes, I know responding God's way can be extremely challenging at times, especially when "John" is attacking you, and you want to attack him back. But you must realize that John is being influenced by a greater force beyond what you can see. *"For we wrestle not against flesh and blood, but against principalities, against powers, against the rulers of the darkness of this world, against spiritual wickedness in high places"* (**Ephesians 6:12**). Basically, we need to look beyond the person who's attacking us and understand who is the real culprit. There are other forces at work and "John" is being influenced by these powers, knowingly or unknowingly. The goal of your opposition is to provoke anger and hinder your purpose in life. Look beyond the person.

We will always have adversaries that come to destroy our focus and credibility. If they are successful, it can affect our influence and the impact we have on others. That's why it's crucial for us to tame our tongues. Please be mindful of the words that you release from your mouth. Your future depends on it. Once those words leave your mouth, you can't take them back. Use wisdom. Don't give your adversaries an opportunity to discredit who you are. You are God's representative!

Taming your tongue won't be easy at times, but you can do it. You just have to choose to speak things that are beneficial to your life and the lives of others. Practice speaking well of others. Refuse to be a gossip, and learn to speak the truth in love. Gossip usually turns into slander, and it's not pleasing to God. Slander can be very damaging to individuals. You want to build people up, not tear them down.

SLANDERING/GOSSIPING

Slander is telling lies and making false statements about others with the intent of hurting their reputation or character. Slander can destroy lives and ruin relationships. That's why the Bible speaks against this type of behavior. Defamation can cause a great deal of damage to its victims; so, don't do it. You wouldn't want anyone to assassinate your character; therefore, treat others the way you would like to be treated. I noticed that slander is included in the Ten Commandments listed in the Old Testament. According to **Exodus 20:16**, *"Thou shalt not bear false witness against thy neighbor."*

Spreading information that is not true about someone else is considered "bearing false witness." When you slander and speak ill of others, it is considered a sin in the eyes of God. It doesn't represent truth, and anything that is untrue is in opposition to God. Refuse to be a slanderer. Exercise wisdom when engaging in conversations with others. Don't spread malicious lies about other people. And remember, "Whoever conceals hatred with lying lips, and spreads slander is a fool" (**Proverbs 10:18**). Don't be a fool.

Ask yourself, "What do I have to gain by relaying false information about another person?" Honestly, from my experience, you don't gain anything. We'll never reap good fruit by tearing others down. Let me ask you a question. Do you envy the person you are slandering? Are you insecure? Are you jealous of their accomplishments? These are vital questions that need to be answered if you're in the habit of slandering other people.

Slandering is not a wise practice, and I advise you not to participate in it. Why do we feel the need to degrade others to feel better about ourselves? It's time we answer these questions and get to the root cause of our issues. I believe when we spread rumors about others, it says more about our character and less about them. How we treat other people is a reflection of who we truly are.

Ziad K. Abdelnour, President, and CEO of Blackhawk Partners Incorporated stated, "Sometimes people try to expose what's wrong with you because they can't handle what's right about you." What a powerful statement. We must first admit that we have issues and allow God to help us. You can't change what you're not willing to confront. A person that continuously slander other individuals has some underlying issues that need resolving. It's time to work on yourself.

Sometimes when we speak the truth about someone, we don't consider it to be gossip. But I disagree. When you spread harmful and damaging information about someone— whether true or not— you are gossiping. Just because the information is accurate doesn't permit you to share intimate details about another person's life. It's not right. We've all been guilty of chattering about others on some level at some point in our lives, but hopefully, we've matured from such behavior. If not, it's time to grow up and control your tongue.

I've learned that a person who always gossips about others cannot be trusted. If they talk about their friends behind their back, they will surely talk about you behind your back. Avoid confiding anything in these types of people because they will share your private information without your consent. According to **Proverbs 11:13**, "*A talebearer reveals secrets: but he who is trustworthy conceals a matter.*" This text is simply saying that a gossiper will tell everything, but a trustworthy person will keep a secret. Refuse to spread rumors about other individuals; it's not godly. And avoid associating with people who find joy in demeaning and slandering others.

No one has ever become a real success in life by tearing other people down. It doesn't bring you joy and peace. Destroying others is not how you win in life. You'll never be all that God has intended you to be with this kind of behavior. We should have a desire to help, support, encourage, and uplift one another. That is God's desire for each of us. The words you speak and the actions you display should enhance your life and the people you encounter. I like the anonymous quote that says, "We navigate our whole lives using words. Change and improve the words, and I believe that we can change and improve lives." Tame your tongue!

Questions for Discussion & Reflection:

1. After reading this chapter, what insight did you gain as it relates to taming your tongue?

2. Why is it so important that we bridle our tongue? What are the consequences of not taming your tongue?

3. How should we use our words? How have your words helped others recently?

4. What does the bible say about unwholesome and corrupt language?

5. What is the meaning of slander?

6. Do you gossip about others? If so, why? How can you improve in this area?

7. How does controlling your tongue benefit your life?

CHAPTER 14

DISCOVERING YOUR PURPOSE

One of my strongest convictions about life is that you and I have a duty and responsibility to discover our God-given purpose in this lifetime. Everyone has a unique calling that needs to be fulfilled before they leave this earth. Your purpose is the divine assignment that has been given to you by God, and your job is to discover it— and complete it. Your purpose in life is the reason you exist. Everything that God created— He created for a purpose. The Bible declares, *"The Lord has made everything for his own purposes…"* (**Proverbs 16:4**).

Have you ever thought about the reason you exist on planet earth? Well, if you haven't, now is a great time to start. It's time to start thinking about the divine mission that God has created you to accomplish in this lifetime. There are specific tasks that God has formed each of us to do, and we have been endowed with everything we need to fulfill those assignments. In the book <u>Tru: An American Princess</u>, Linda Trimble states, *"When you were born, your purpose was already established. Your abilities, gifts, and talents are already inside. They are a part of your genetic makeup.* " It's time for you to discover your purpose and make your contribution to the world.

YOUR CONTRIBUTION

We all have something to contribute to the society that will improve and enhance the condition of mankind. Your contribution is your purpose. When you find your purpose, you will find what you need to contribute to this world. It's imperative that we strive to make an impact in the lives of others every opportunity we're afforded. Are you making your contribution? If you fail to do your part, someone is deprived of your influence. You have the power to make a difference in a person's life. So, do it! Let's not rise every morning as if we were here by accident— moving about our day on autopilot. That's not living; that's existing.

Live on purpose. Wake up every morning with purpose on your mind. Be intentional about how you spend your day. God desires for us to live an abundant life. Jesus states, *"The thief cometh not, but for to steal, and to kill, and to destroy: I come that they might have life, and that they might have it more abundantly"* (**John 10:10**).

When you discover purpose, you live a fulfilling and satisfying existence. It feels good to be a part of something that's greater than yourself. We experience great joy when we offer our gifts and talents to the world and help improve humanity. That's why it's extremely important that we discover our life's work. The late Dr. Myles Munroe, an author, speaker, educator, leadership mentor, and consultant stated, "When purpose is not known, abuse is inevitable." Basically, if you don't know the purpose of your life, abuse is unavoidable. I wholeheartedly agree with this concept. If you fail to discover your true calling in life, you will abuse your life and allow others to abuse you as well.

ABUSE IS INEVITABLE

People will assign you a purpose that did not come from your creator if you don't find it for yourself. Also, if you don't understand why God created you, you will not only abuse yourself, but there's potential to abuse others as well. Several years ago, I didn't know my purpose or why God created me; therefore, I abused my life by engaging in excessive gambling, alcohol addiction, prescription pill abuse, and other bad habits. During this season of my life, I was unaware of my true identity. As for as I was concerned, I had no purpose. When I think back on this painful time of my life, I realize that I was abusing my mind, my body, my time, my finances, and my opportunities—all because I didn't know the purpose of my existence. I genuinely believe I wouldn't have chosen to abuse my life if I had known my purpose.

After experiencing those challenging years of my life, I now understand that we are made for a purpose and designed for destiny. I know that God gives us identity and our lives are meaningful. We are not here by accident. God wants to do some amazing things through us—if we allow Him to. When you know your purpose, it leads and disciplines your life. Purpose gives you a vision for your life. It governs your relationships and dictates your choices. Your vision tells you who to connect with and who to avoid. When your purpose is leading your life, it dictates what habits you can and cannot form. It can be a powerful guiding force in our lives when we discover it. Find your purpose!

Let's take it a step further. If you don't know the purpose of the people that God has positioned in your life, you will abuse them or even lose them. It's essential to understand the purpose of the people who are in your life. Your relationships are your most valuable assets. Do you know the purpose of your spouse, children, friends, job, supervisors, and family members? I honestly believe that God connects us with certain people who serve a purpose in our lives. Don't take your relationships for granted. God has placed special people in your path for a specific purpose, and it's your job to discover why. I call these encounters divine connections.

Once you gain an understanding of your own purpose in life, you're able to discern the purpose of the people God has placed in your path. Everything that God accomplishes in our lives is for a reason. God has already planned our lives. He can speak our future to us before it happens; He knows our end from the beginning. God is intentional and purposeful. There are no coincidences with Him. **Isaiah 46:9-10** asserts, *"Remember the former things, those of long ago; I am God, and there is no other; I am God, and there is none like me. I make known the end from the beginning, from ancient times, what is still to come. I say, My purpose will stand, and I will do all that I please."*

I want to reiterate that God had "purpose" on his mind when He created you. And that means you don't have the burden of trying to create a purpose for your life. It has already been established for you by the creator. You just need to discover it!

GOD'S PLAN

God designed a plan for your life before you entered the world (**Jeremiah 1:5**). He wants to use your life to bring Him glory in the earth realm. What an honor to be chosen by God to do His work on planet earth. We are chosen vessels— created to do good works—which was confirmed before the foundation of the world. In **Ephesians 2:10**, Paul states, *"For we are His workmanship, created in Christ Jesus for good works, which God prepared beforehand that we should walk in them."*

Create a plan based on what you believe God wants you to do in this season of your life. Don't look to others for a plan, but seek God about the plan and purpose He has for your life. He is your Creator, and only the Creator knows the intent of His creation. In **Jeremiah 29:11**, God spoke, *"For I know the thoughts that I think toward you, saith the Lord, thoughts of peace, and not of evil, to give you an expected end."* Remember, people can't give you purpose. They can confirm your purpose, but they can't give you purpose. Your purpose was already established before you entered the earth. Only God can give us meaning and purpose because He designed us.

God has designed a great life for you, and if you follow His blueprint, you will reach your intended destination. He has already equipped you with everything you need to do His special work. You have the necessary tools, parts, and components to operate and function in your purpose. The tools that you need to operate in your calling are the gifts endowed to you by the creator. We were all awarded gifts that were assigned to us before we entered the earth.

GIFTS & TALENTS

Everyone has inherent gifts, talents, and abilities that were granted to them by God. Our gifts are the tools that we must use to fulfill our purpose, but we have to discover what those gifts are.

Understanding your gifts and talents will help you to discover your true calling in life. Start paying attention to the things you love to do. What drives you? What excites you? What fulfills you, and makes you come alive? What are you passionate about? Passion is usually connected to purpose. Answering these questions is essential to discovering your true purpose in life.

Discovering your gifts and talents are clues to knowing the "why" behind your existence. You must be willing to study yourself and observe your life. Sometimes we expend time and energy studying everyone else's life and not our own. Try to be more concerned with yourself, and focus on what God has called you to do. Remember, everyone has a responsibility to fulfill their God-given assignment while here on earth. If you have not identified your gifts and talents, now is a great time to start. You may need to step out of your comfort zone and try something different. You have untapped treasures that are hidden or the inside of you waiting to be discovered. It would be a tragedy to leave this world and never use your gifts for a higher purpose.

Once you discover your gifts, you have a responsibility to develop and refine them. This can be done through training, volunteering, seminars, mentorship, and higher education. Maximize your gifts, and continue to hone your skills. Remember, your gifts are the tools you'll use to operate and function in your purpose. *"A man's gift maketh room for him, and bringeth him*

231

before great men" (**Proverbs 18:16**). Our gifts and talents will open doors for us and connect us with people that we would never have met without discovering our gifts.

When you continue to improve your talents and refine your gifts, you are adding value to yourself. It is imperative that you master your skills. And when you do, people will begin to gravitate toward you and seek out your services. Your expertise will be in high demand because you decided to enhance your abilities. You have something unique to offer this world, and it's time for you to identify it. This world needs what you have. We cannot make our contribution to society if we don't know what we possess. That's why it's vital that you discover your gifts— so you can fulfill your assignment. Your purpose is not always apparent; therefore, you need to pray that God will give you an understanding of His plan for your life.

SMALL BEGINNINGS

You could very well be moving in purpose right now and not even recognize it. Just because it doesn't feel like you're in purpose doesn't mean you're not. If you're living your life according to God's design, that's all that matters. You're going to have some good days and some bad days, but continue to follow the path that God has placed before you. The place you're in at this moment may be dreadful; however, it could be the very place that's intended to prepare you and launch you into your divine purpose. Embrace your current season. Learn all that you can, and don't discount or discredit the place you're in right now. The Bible teaches us to not despise the day of small and humble beginnings (**Zechariah 4:10**). We shouldn't take our early seasons for granted. Our difficult and challenging beginnings allow us to appreciate our successes in the long run.

Many great people started in small places. There are a vast number of great ideas that originated from humble beginnings. So, as I mentioned earlier, embrace the early stages of your journey. Yes, you will have difficult moments and challenging seasons, but they're all a part of the plan. Learn from your mistakes; gain wisdom from your errors. Every season you encounter is preparing you for the future. If you're currently experiencing adversity, perhaps you're under construction right now. God is shaping you and molding your character, preparing you for the next level of your purpose. He is purging you, pruning you, and refining your life to do His great work. It's all about perspective. Everything that's taking place in your life is working together for your good, and God will make sure of it (**Rom 8:28**). You must believe this if you plan on accomplishing your divine purpose.

Some situations arise in our lives that we have no control over, but we must keep our eyes on the prize. Focus on the vision. It's not about what happens to you; it's how you respond to what happens to you. Your response determines your outcome, and it also determines whether you are promoted or not. Control how you react to the people and circumstances that may offend you. Attitude is everything. It can help you or hinder your elevation in life.

When you're aware of your calling, everything you do needs to line up with that mission. If it doesn't line up with your vision, it's a distraction. Be mindful of the people you entertain, the events you attend, and the projects you involve yourself with. Surround yourself with individuals who have a sense of purpose and a desire to shift their lives to the next level. If you're not attentive to who you connect with, those people will become a distraction in your life.

DISTRACTIONS

According to the Cambridge English Dictionary, a distraction is something that prevents you from giving full attention to something else. It will take you off course and pull you in a different direction— away from what you need to be focused on presently. Be keenly aware of distractions because they are the enemy of your purpose. The purpose of a distraction is to distract you from your purpose. Whenever you become aware of your purpose in life, expect opposition and distractions to appear frequently.

When you say, "I know my calling," distraction says, "I'm on my way." When you say, "I'm pursuing my purpose," opposition says, "Here I come, I'm knocking at your door." It comes with the territory. Don't be alarmed; just remain conscious of your surroundings. Always keep the assignment at the forefront, and you will overcome any opposition that shows up in your life.

Always remember your mission. Engage in activities that are conducive to your mission in life. Are your current endeavors shifting you closer to your destiny? You may be doing something good right now, but doing a 'good thing' is not always the 'best thing' for your life. A "good" thing could be distracting you from doing a "God" thing. I like the verse in the Bible that says, *"All things are lawful for me, but all things are not expedient: all things are lawful for me, but all things edify not"* (**1 Corinthians 10:23**). In this text, the writer Paul is saying that the things you desire may not be wrong, they may not be a sin, but are they beneficial for your life? Do they line up with the vision God has placed in your heart?

What are your desires? Do you aspire to fulfill your calling in life? Are your current deeds contributing to your purpose in life? These are the questions you have to ask yourself. And be honest with yourself about where you are right now. If you're not on the path to purpose, it's time to seek God and get on board. Refuse to do the "good" thing, and do the "best" thing for your life in this season. Thomas Merton, an American Catholic writer, and theologian asserted, "People may spend their whole lives climbing the ladder of success only to find, once they reach the top, that the ladder is leaning against the wrong wall." You don't want to arrive at the end of your life and realize that you have followed the wrong path, the wrong dreams, and the wrong purpose. What a tragedy!

Remember, there will always be distractions. Do not allow the disruptions of this world to lure you away from the plan that God has formulated for your life. We don't have to look very far; distractions are everywhere. The TV, radio, social media, kids, family drama, and friends are all potential distractions. Fight against these disruptions, and focus on creating a legacy for your family and future generations. When we operate in our purpose, our children have a higher chance of fulfilling their purpose. It's always great when children can observe other family members following their dreams and achieving greatness. It gives them confidence and a belief that they can perform as well. Become a great role model for your family; decide to walk in your God-given purpose. And yes, everyone is watching you— whether you realize it or not.

WALKING IN PURPOSE

Once you've decided to step into purpose, power is a by-product of that decision. One definition of the word power is a person with authority. So again, once you've made a decision to walk in purpose, you have taken authority over your life. You have taken authority over your choices, habits, words, attitudes, and the manner in which you conduct your life. You are in control of your destiny.

Power is also described as having influence; therefore, once you've decided to walk in purpose, you possess influence. When you're walking in your purpose, you influence others to pursue their purpose as well, and you inspire them to live a Godly existence. Influence is a great responsibility. We can influence others for the better or for worse. Of course, our goal should be to influence others positively. Use your influence to steer people toward a Godly lifestyle.

When I think about purpose, power, and influence, I think about Christ. He is one of our greatest examples. He came to the earth over two-thousand years ago to serve a purpose, and He fulfilled that purpose. Jesus was born to die; His destination was the cross. Die for what? He died for the "remission of our sins" and to reconcile us back to God (**Matthew 26:28; 2 Corinthians 5:18**). Jesus desires for us to live an abundant life. He announces,

237

"...My purpose is to give them a rich and satisfying life" (**John 10:10**).

Christ walked in authority, and He taught with conviction while He was here on earth. In the Bible, it explains, *"And it came to pass, when Jesus had ended these sayings, the people were astonished at his doctrine: For he taught them as one having authority, and not as the scribes"* (**Matthew 7:28-29).** Christ also had influence. The Bible records how large crowds followed Him wherever he would go. Why? Because Jesus walked in purpose. He knew who He was, and He stayed focused on His assignment. Jesus is our model.

Allow me to pose this question once again. Are you doing what God has called you to do in this season? If you're not currently walking in purpose, here are some crucial questions I need you to ponder. Ask yourself, "Why am I here?" "What was I created to do?" "What am I passionate about?" "What is my assignment?" "Is there more to life than just existing?" Now, you might not know the answer to these questions right away, but it's a start. It's time for you to meditate on these key questions and seek God for answers. Once you do this, you've made the first step toward discovering the reason for your existence. It's impossible to be truly fulfilled in life when you're clueless about your purpose.

After observing my life and the life of others, I've discovered something. If you desire to prevail, to be powerful, successful, and live a fulfilled life, then you must walk in your purpose. And if you want to know your purpose, you have to pursue God. You must pray, seek, chase, study, and follow God. Build a close and intimate relationship with Him. As I mentioned earlier, He is your creator, and you are His creation. God knows the intent of His creation. He created you for a reason, and He wants to reveal to you the plan that He has established for your life.

PURSUE GOD'S DESIGN

I know many of us have created plans for our future, but if we desire for God to be committed to our plans, we need to make sure our intentions line up with His design for our lives. Seek God about your future before you make any grand decisions. His purpose should always override your plans because His plan is the best plan. Follow His purpose. God always knows best. The Bible declares, "*Many are the plans in a person's heart, but it is the Lord's purpose that prevails*" (**Proverbs 19:21**). God's intended design for your life will exceed anything you can imagine. Trust Him with your life. You will not be disappointed. One thing I know for sure is that God's purpose will always prosper— guaranteed.

Please understand that I'm not suggesting that we never make plans for our future. Of course, we need strategies, goals, visions, and aspirations; however, before we make elaborate plans, I suggest that we seek the wisdom and heart of God about our destiny. Our life is at stake. We don't want to waste time pursuing the wrong things in life. Remember, you only get one life; so, let's make the best use of it. I agree with the quote by Benjamin Franklin, one of the Founding Fathers of the United States, that says, "If you fail to plan, you are planning to fail." We must have plans!

Once you discover your purpose, you'll begin to experience a life of joy, fulfillment, contentment, and satisfaction. Your focus will change, and your perspective on life will eventually evolve. As you grow and develop, you'll have opportunities to help improve the life of others as well. Remember, it's impossible to enhance others if you're not improving yourself.

My hope is for you to discover your God-given purpose, and when you do—pursue it passionately. Become the person that God has destined you to be. It's time to shift to the next level!

Questions for Discussion & Reflection:

1. After reading this chapter, what insight did you gain as it relates to discovering your purpose?

2. Why is it so important for you to discover your calling in life? What are the consequences of not finding your purpose?

3. Do you know your God-given purpose? If not, what steps will you take to discover it?

4. What are your gifts, talents, and special abilities?

5. Why is it imperative for you to identify your gifts and talents? What role do they play as it relates to your purpose in life?

6. What are distractions? How can they hinder you from fulfilling your purpose?

7. Do you have a plan for your future? Do your plans align with God's plan for your life?

8. How often do you seek God about His design for your life? What will you do differently after reading this chapter?

Next Level Living

CHAPTER 15

CONCLUSION: NEXT LEVEL LIVING

When we embody the attributes that are outlined in this book, we'll experience the abundant life that God desires for each of us—a life of fulfillment and satisfaction. My goal in writing this book is to enhance and improve the lives of others by sharing information that has been instrumental to my growth and progress. A concept that I believe to be true is that if we're not growing, we're dying; if we're not progressing, we're regressing; and if we're not getting better, we're getting worse.

The principles revealed in this book will help you to make progress in every aspect of your life, but you must take action. If you incorporate these principles into your everyday routine, your life will shift to new levels— guaranteed.

It's difficult to shift to the next phase of your life when you don't have accurate knowledge. This is the position I was in before I learned the principles that I expounded on in the previous chapters. My life was insane. I continued to do the same things expecting different results. It was time to change, but I didn't know how. So, I became a seeker. This journey of self-discovery has reformed and revolutionized my life. The perspective I have on life is so much richer, and I possess an internal peace that surpasses all human understanding. I can honestly say that my transformation is a result of my seeking and finding truth.

When you don't know the truth, how can you apply it to your life, and make the necessary changes? It's impossible. For you to grow and become the individual that God has destined you to become, you must obtain knowledge. If you know better, you have an opportunity to do better. The principles and truths revealed in this book will help bring real change to your life. You can live a life that's unrecognizable if you're willing to put in the effort that it takes to make real change. Only the truth will set you free and allow you to move forward in life. God's desire is for you to prosper in every aspect of your life, and you need to have this same desire for yourself.

After studying the attributes and principles noted in the previous chapters (character, love, honor, humility, and forgiveness), I made a decision that I was going to incorporate these principles into my daily existence. My life was going nowhere, and I was in desperate need of change. I was in bondage to many bad habits for years; however, once I began to work the principles outlined in this book, the trajectory of my life altered. I hope that you will take hold of these concepts and incorporate them into your life. Growth only takes place when you begin to walk out the knowledge you have obtained. I urge you to practice what you have learned; otherwise, there will be no elevation.

While walking out these principles, you'll begin to discover your true identity and the reason you exist on this earth. There are people and things that will no longer be of interest to you once you begin to feed your mind the truth. Your perspective on life will change, and you will start removing people and things that are not conducive to your growth process. This is great because once you remove bad habits, people, and other things that are not beneficial to your life, you open the door for the right things to come in. You have clarity now. Sometimes we have to eliminate certain people and things to get a clear picture of who we are and what we need in our lives.

Back when I started my transformational journey, there were many people and things that I had to remove from my life to become who I am today. Now, I'm not saying that I have arrived, nor am I saying that I'm perfect—but I 'm very thankful for my journey and how far I've come. This journey has not been easy, and I'm sure you can say the same about your life. When I removed the unnecessary people and bad habits that were hindering my progress, I discovered my identity and my purpose in life. This did not happen swiftly, but if you remain persistent, growth is inevitable. I continue to put in the effort required for my growth and development. And I want you to do the same.

My desire is for you to become a lifetime learner. I want you to be dedicated to improving your life. The principles outlined in this book are fundamental to me, and I truly believe they are essential to living a peaceful and fulfilled existence. They are the foundation by which I live my life. I have a passion for growth and development. We must grow if we intend to become the person God has created us to be. No growth, no elevation. Fulfilling your God-given purpose without development and maturity is impossible. Strive to grow in every area of your life.

The values summarized in this book have assisted me physically, mentally, spiritually, emotionally, and relationally. I hope they will do the same for you because that was my intention for writing this book. If you have a desire to help others, then you must help yourself first. Paulo Coelho, a Brazilian lyricist, and novelist state, "If you conquer yourself, then you conquer the world." It all starts with you. Develop the discipline you need to enhance your life, and then you can do the same for others. You have to be the change you want to see in others. Start with yourself!

Conquering yourself is the key to living a life of freedom and serenity. If you're not free, you can't possibly help others become free. But when you've been delivered, you can assist other individuals in their deliverance process. Remember, we have to deal with the bondage that's in our own lives in order to help liberate the next person.

Freedom comes with a price. You must be willing to pay the cost to walk in freedom. The cost associated with freedom is being willing to do what it takes to change your life. For example, you must walk in love, humility, honor, forgiveness, and excellence just to name a few. If you fail to uphold these standards, you will not experience a joyful and peaceful existence. Trust me, I know from personal experience. I had to seek out the truth, and allow God to help me transform my thinking. Now, I'm in a position to share my wisdom in the hopes of enhancing the lives of others.

We can only enrich others when our lives are advancing and improving. Never stop learning and growing because we'll never know it all. Your goal should be to evolve until your life comes to an end. God's wisdom is infinite, and it will take us a lifetime to discover our true identity. There are layers to who we are; therefore, there's always more to learn. Maintain a teachable spirit, and keep your heart open to correction from others. We can learn from anyone if we just maintain an open heart. Sometimes pride can prevent us from seeking advice and asking for help when we need it the most. Please don't fall into the pride trap. When you're receptive to other's knowledge and experiences, it will enhance your life immensely. Don't be prideful!

After reading this book, I hope you have gained valuable insight into what steps you need to take to initiate your transformation process. Remember, you will need the grace of God to help you overcome the many challenges that arise. Keep God first in your life, and He will help you create a life that will be unrecognizable. God is not a respecter of persons; therefore, if He helped me, He will do the same for you. Today, I challenge you to surrender your old way of thinking and your old way of functioning in life. Embrace God's way of living by incorporating the principles and standards written in this book. When you do, your life will never be the same.

As you begin your transformational journey, be willing to endure the process that God takes you through. It will not be easy, but it's worth it. If you plan on moving to the next phase of your life, you have to be willing to grow and develop. No exceptions! There will be seasons that are uncomfortable and challenging; however, they are necessary for your next level. Remain optimistic and keep a positive outlook. Maintaining the right attitude is the key to promotion and a peaceful existence. Sometimes you have to check yourself to make sure you're not in your own way. You don't want to stop your own progress.

Examine yourself! Don't become your own worst enemy. Keep the faith, and believe that you can evolve into the person God has destined you to become. Remain dedicated to your growth process. And you will reap the rewards.

I hope this book has inspired and motivated you to initiate your journey of self-discovery and purpose. It's time to challenge yourself to greatness, and refuse to live an ordinary existence. Once you incorporate these divine principles into your routine, your outlook and behavior will begin to reflect the nature of God. When this happens, you'll eventually walk in divine favor, influencing others everywhere you go.

Maintain the qualities of honor, integrity, humility, excellence, and mercy. Upholding these Godly standards will invite blessings into your life, and allow you to reach your destiny. I live my life by the principles noted above, and I encourage you to do the same. When you stand firm for the truth no matter what, you'll excel in every area of your life. This is next level living!

Next Level Living

About the Author

Dr. Tamika Ford is a native of Shreveport, LA. She is a devoted Christian that desires to live out her life's purpose. Dr. Ford is the founder of "Freedom in Truth," a non-profit organization established in 2016. She is also the founder of "Single and Saved" and "Women in Purpose" ministries.

Dr. Ford is dedicated to the work and call of God on her life. She overcame many obstacles, bondages, and addictions in her life through the power and grace of God. Dr. Ford is also the author of a book entitled, "_Single and Saved: Embracing your Season of Singleness_." Her greatest conviction is that everyone has a duty and obligation to discover their identity, and fulfill their God-given purpose while here on earth.

To order copies of this book or previous book(s) (*Single and Saved..*), go to www.tamikaford.com or contact Dr. Tamika Ford at fordtamika79@gmail.com, or by phone at 318-612-0437.

Book Dr. Ford for your upcoming events at www.singleandsavedlife.net/speaking or contact by phone at 318-612-0437. Thank you for your support!!!

www.ingramcontent.com/pod-product-compliance
Lightning Source LLC
Chambersburg PA
CBHW030920090426
42737CB00007B/257